SEASONS IN THE HOME

SPRING

CREATIVE
HOME
ARTS
—CLUB—

CREATIVE HOME ARTS LIBRARY™

SPR

ING

CREATIVE
HOME
ARTS
— CLUB —

CREATIVE HOME ARTS CLUB
MINNETONKA, MINNESOTA

CREDITS

SEASONS IN THE HOME
SPRING

Printed in 2006.

Tom Carpenter
Creative Director

Heather Koshiol
Managing Editor

Jennifer Weaverling
Senior Book Development Coordinator

Jenya Prosmitsky
Book Design & Production

3 4 5 6 7 8 / 09 08 07 06
ISBN 1-58159-224-8
© 2004 Creative Home Arts Club

Creative Home Arts Club
12301 Whitewater Drive
Minnetonka, Minnesota 55343
www.creativehomeartsclub.com

Contributing Writers

Mary Evans
Lisa Golden Schroeder
Zoe Graul
Ethel Hofman
Patsy Jamieson
Michele Anna Jordan
Sue Jorgensen
Colleen Miner
Cheryl Nelson
Yula Nelson
Maggie Oster
Barbara Pleasant
Kathleen Prisant
Mark Scarbrough
John Schumacher
Bruce Weinstein

Contributing Photographers

Phil Aarrestad
Bill Lindner
Mark Macemon
Tad Ware

Additional Photography

Bill Adams
Jim Block
David Cavagnaro
Walter Chandoha
Crandall & Crandall
Todd Davis
Joseph DeSciose
Linda and Alan Detrick
Derek Fell
Marge Garfield
Saxon Holt
Maggie Oster
Jerry Pavia
Robert Perron
Barbara Pleasant
Joseph Strautch, Jr.

Special thanks to: Mike Billstein, Terry Casey, Janice Cauley, Matt Dillon, Sandy Zilka.

CONTENTS

SPRING

INTRODUCTION

Awakening. Rebirth. Buds. Blossoms. Life. Sun. Warmth. There are hundreds of ways to describe spring. But roll them all together and one word captures the essence of it all: Joy.

Depending on where you live, winter might be long and rough, short and uneventful, or somewhere in between. But we can all relate to the anticipation of what's going to come: Spring! And that brings joy to anybody's heart — especially Creative Home Arts Club Members like you, people who are just itching to get their creative juices flowing again (much like the sap of spring), and their hands busy making beautiful creations of all kinds.

That's what *Seasons in the Home — Spring* is all about! Here are hundreds of ideas for making the most of this most-appreciated season.

Find dozens of easy and intriguing recipes that celebrate the season's fresh bounty.

With your energy and creativity at high tide, this is the perfect time for crafting creativity. The ideas and instructions you need are right here.

Spring and decorating go hand in hand. Discover wonderful ideas for home makeovers!

Everybody likes to play in the spring dirt, so we walk you through gardening projects that offer both flavor and color.

And, Easter and nice weather call for gatherings with friends and family. Here are easy, complete menus.

It's time to bring the joy of spring to both your home and your heart. Let *Seasons in the Home — Spring* be the guidebook for your creativity-filled journey.

S P R I N G

COOKING

Spring cooking has a taste all its own: Fresh. Light. Vibrant. Lively. Spring cooking also has a theme: Easy. Simple. Fun. Fast. Those are the kinds of recipes we're proud to present to you within the pages of this chapter. So create wonderful breakfasts, appetizers, brunches, lunches, main dishes, side dishes, salads and desserts … and still have time to enjoy everything else that life — and spring — has to offer.

Facing page: Aunt Hanni's Blueberry Torte, page 50

Pancakes

Even the best mixes can't compare to pancakes made the old-fashioned way and eaten hot from the skillet on a cool spring morning. If you don't have buttermilk, add 2 teaspoons lemon juice or white vinegar to 1 cup milk and let stand at room temperature for 5 minutes without stirring.

1	cup all-purpose flour
2	teaspoons sugar
1½	teaspoons baking powder
½	teaspoon salt
1	egg
1	cup buttermilk
3	tablespoons vegetable oil

1 In medium bowl, stir together flour, sugar, baking powder and salt.

2 Make well in center. Add egg, buttermilk and 1 tablespoon of the oil; whisk until smooth.

3 Pour remaining 2 tablespoons oil into large skillet. Heat over medium-high heat until hot.

4 Pour ¼ cup batter into skillet. When bubbles appear and burst on surface, flip over and continue cooking about 1 to 2 minutes until underside is golden brown.

5 Serve hot with sweet butter and maple or fruit syrups, if desired.

15 (3-inch) pancakes.
Preparation time: 15 minutes.
Ready to serve: 25 minutes.
Per serving: 105 calories, 5 g fat (1 g saturated fat), 25 mg cholesterol, 215 mg sodium, 0.5 g fiber.

Variations

- **Apple-Raisin Pancakes**
  Fold 1 unpeeled chopped apple and ¼ cup raisins into batter.

- **Blueberry-Ginger Pancakes**
  Toss 1 cup blueberries with ½ teaspoon ground ginger; fold into batter.

- **Pineapple-Walnut Pancakes**
  Combine ¼ cup drained crushed pineapple with ⅓ cup chopped walnuts; fold into batter.

- **Crisp Bacon Pancakes**
  Omit sugar; stir ½ cup crumbled crisp cooked bacon into batter.

- **Southern Cornmeal Pancakes**
  Omit sugar, decrease flour to ½ cup and add ½ cup cornmeal; fold in ½ cup cooked or canned corn to batter.

- **Cheddar Cheese Pancakes**
  Omit sugar; stir 1 cup (4 oz.) shredded cheddar cheese and 1 teaspoon dried parsley into batter.

Chef's Note

- For speed and ease, combine the dry ingredients for 4 recipes of pancakes. Store in an airtight container in a cool, dry place — not the refrigerator. When needed, add wet ingredients for 1 recipe (1 egg, 1 cup buttermilk plus 1 tablespoon vegetable oil) to 1 cup plus 1 tablespoon of the dry mixture.

Smoked Salmon and Olive Quiche

The savory egg-cheese pie hails from the Alsace-Lorraine region of France. The popular *Quiche Lorraine* is a pastry shell with crisp bacon bits folded into a savory custard filling before baking. Almost any vegetables and/or meats may be used, as in this version. Make a couple quiches; enjoy one and freeze the other.

1	(9-inch) pie shell
6	(1-oz.) slices *Sima's Gravlax* (page 17)
3	tablespoons chopped ripe olives
2 to 3	tablespoons capers, rinsed
3	eggs
1	cup milk
2	tablespoons sour cream
	Dash ground white pepper

1 Heat oven to 350°F.

2 Prick bottom and sides of pie shell with fork. Bake 5 minutes.

3 Place 1½ teaspoons chopped olives on each salmon slice. Roll up as for jelly roll. Arrange in wagon wheel pattern on bottom of pie shell. Sprinkle with capers.

4 In medium bowl, whisk eggs, milk, sour cream and pepper. Pour over salmon.

5 Place on baking sheet. Bake 45 minutes or until toothpick inserted near center comes out clean. Serve warm or at room temperature.

6 servings.
Preparation time: 20 minutes.
Ready to serve: 1 hour, 5 minutes.
Per serving: 165 calories, 10 g fat (3 g saturated fat), 95 mg cholesterol, 290 mg sodium, 0.5 g fiber.

Variation

- **Tomato and Roasted Garlic Quiche**
Add 2 chopped tomatoes and ½ cup shredded garlic-flavored cheddar cheese to egg mixture. Bake as directed above.

PINEAPPLE AND BROWN SUGAR STRATA

Easy and fuss-free, this is a great dish for a spring brunch. Assemble it the night before, cover and refrigerate. Then 45 minutes before serving, slip the strata into a preheated oven and bake as directed below.

8 tablespoons butter
1 cup packed brown sugar
1 (20-oz.) can crushed pineapple, drained, juice reserved
4 eggs
3 sourdough English muffins, torn into 1-inch pieces
½ cup quick-cooking oats
2 tablespoons grated orange peel

1 Heat oven to 375°F.

2 In large bowl, beat 6 tablespoons of the butter and ¾ cup of the brown sugar at medium speed until fluffy. Spread mixture over bottom of 9-inch deep dish pie pan.

3 Spread pineapple over brown sugar mixture. Set aside.

4 In another large bowl, whisk together eggs and reserved pineapple juice. Add sourdough muffin pieces; press down to soak. Pour over crushed pineapple.

5 In small bowl, cut oatmeal, orange peel and remaining ¼ cup brown sugar into remaining 2 tablespoons butter until mixture crumbles. Sprinkle over pie.

6 Bake 40 minutes or until bubbly at sides. Serve warm.

8 servings.
Preparation time: 25 minutes.
Ready to serve: 1 hour, 5 minutes.
Per serving: 355 calories, 15 g fat (8 g saturated fat), 135 mg cholesterol, 220 mg sodium, 1.5 g fiber.

GRILLED ANTIPASTI WITH NO-FUSS AIOLI

Kick off a springtime barbecue with a plate of antipasti, those marinated vegetables so popular in Italian cooking. Aioli is an uncooked garlic sauce made with oil and eggs, but here it's made with mayonnaise for simplicity.

Aioli
1½   cups mayonnaise
3   garlic cloves or to taste, crushed
1   tablespoon lemon juice
1   tablespoon Dijon mustard
1   teaspoon salt
½   teaspoon freshly ground pepper

Vegetables
1   medium red onion, sliced into ½-inch-thick rings
1   medium fennel bulb, trimmed, cut into ¼-inch-thick slices
1   lb. asparagus spears, trimmed
2   red bell peppers, cut into 1-inch-thick strips
2   (6-oz.) zucchini, cut lengthwise into long ¼-inch-thick slices
12   canned artichoke bottoms
1   (8-oz.) bottle Italian dressing
8   sprigs rosemary, soaked in water 30 minutes, then drained

1 For Aioli: In medium bowl, mix mayonnaise, garlic, lemon juice, Dijon, salt and pepper until smooth. Cover; refrigerate until ready to serve. Aioli can be prepared ahead. Store, covered, in refrigerator up to 5 days.

2 For Vegetables: Place red onion, fennel, asparagus, bell peppers, zucchini and artichokes in large bowl or roasting pan; pour bottled dressing over. Turn to coat; marinate at room temperature 30 minutes, tossing frequently.

3 Heat grill for direct cooking. If using gas grill, place rosemary sprigs directly on lava rocks; if using charcoal grill, place directly on high-heat coals.

4 Place red onion and fennel directly over high heat. Cover; grill, turning once, 8 minutes or until golden and soft. Transfer to serving platter.

5 Place asparagus and bell peppers directly over high heat. Cover; grill, turning once, 5 minutes or until browned. Transfer to serving platter.

6 Place zucchini and artichokes directly over high heat. Cover; grill, turning once, 4 minutes or until browned. Transfer to serving platter. Serve with reserved Aioli.

8 servings.
Preparation time: 20 minutes.
Ready to serve: 1 hour, 10 minutes.
Per serving: 380 calories, 36 g total fat (5.5 g saturated fat), 25 mg cholesterol, 715 mg sodium, 4 g fiber.

SPINACH TIMBALES

Timbale refers to the round, high-sided mold that tapers slightly and is used for baking, as well as the dish that is baked in the mold. Timbale molds can be purchased in some specialty cookware stores. Custard cups provide an easier alternative. Using frozen spinach in this recipe speeds the cooking process without sacrificing taste.

Timbales

1	tablespoon butter
¼	cup minced onion
1½	teaspoons minced garlic
1½	teaspoons minced fresh ginger
¼	cup tomato sauce
½	tablespoon coriander
½	teaspoon cumin
¼	teaspoon ground red pepper
¼	teaspoon salt
⅛	teaspoon turmeric
1	(10-oz.) pkg. frozen chopped spinach, thawed
¼	cup (1 oz.) freshly grated Parmesan cheese
¾	cup crème fraîche or buttermilk
3	eggs

Sauce

1	lb. tomatoes, peeled
2	teaspoons finely minced fresh ginger
¼	teaspoon salt

1 Heat oven to 350°F. Spray 6 (6-oz.) custard cups or timbale molds with nonstick cooking spray.

2 Melt butter in medium skillet over medium heat. Add onion, garlic and ginger; sauté 5 to 8 minutes or until browned. Add tomato sauce, coriander, cumin, red pepper, salt and turmeric. Simmer, covered, about 5 minutes or until a film of oil forms on sauce. Squeeze spinach to remove excess moisture; add to tomato sauce. Simmer, covered, 10 minutes. Remove from heat; cool.

3 In food processor, puree spinach mixture. Add cheese; pulse to combine. Add crème fraîche and eggs; puree until smooth.

4 Divide mixture evenly among custard cups. Place in large shallow pan; add enough boiling water to pan to come halfway up sides of molds. Bake about 30 minutes or until spinach just begins to pull away from edges of molds.

5 Meanwhile, puree tomatoes, ginger and salt in food processor to form a slightly chunky sauce. Place in small saucepan; simmer over low heat just until hot.

6 Unmold timbales; serve with tomato sauce.

6 servings.
Preparation time: 25 minutes.
Ready to serve: 1 hour, 10 minutes.
Per serving: 195 calories, 15.5 g total fat (8.5 g saturated fat), 150 mg cholesterol, 435 mg sodium, 2 g fiber.

SIMA'S GRAVLAX

Gravlax — thinly sliced, cured salmon — is very expensive to purchase. But the price is slashed when you prepare gravlax at home with this recipe. It's a great and light way to eat fresh fish in spring!

1 (1½ lb.) boneless salmon fillet
¾ cup kosher (coarse) salt
¼ cup granulated sugar
1 large bunch dill

1 Rinse salmon and pat dry. Set aside.

2 In small bowl, combine salt and sugar; mix well. Spread one-half of the dill in 3-quart casserole; sprinkle with one-half of the salt mixture.

3 Place salmon, skin side down, in casserole. Cover with remaining dill and salt mixtures, pressing mixtures into surface of salmon. Wrap fish tightly with parchment paper, then plastic wrap.

4 Weigh down salmon with 5-lb. weight (you can use a 5-lb. bag of sugar or flour wrapped in a plastic bag.) Refrigerate 2 days, turning once.

5 Unwrap fish; run under cold water to remove dill and salt mixtures. If too salty, soak in cold water 30 minutes; pat dry.

6 With sharp knife, slice salmon paper thin on the diagonal. Serve with fresh slices of lime and crackers.

10 servings.
Preparation time: 30 minutes.
Ready to serve: 2 days.
Per serving: 100 calories, 4 g total fat (1 g saturated fat), 45 mg cholesterol, 1380 g sodium, 0 g fiber.

Chef's Note

- Gravlax may be refrigerated 3 to 4 days. If wrapped tightly, it may be frozen. Move from freezer to refrigerator 24 hours before needed.

SCALLION AND CILANTRO POT STICKERS

Look for wonton skins in the produce or Asian section of large supermarkets, or in specialty food stores.

Pot Stickers

4	tablespoons vegetable oil
1	tablespoon chopped fresh ginger
1	cup chopped green onions, including tender green portion of stem
2½	cups chopped Savoy or Napa cabbage
2	tablespoons soy sauce
⅓	cup chopped cilantro
1½	teaspoons toasted sesame oil
24	wonton skins
⅔	cup water

Dipping Sauce

¼	cup soy sauce
¼	cup orange juice
¼	cup water
2	tablespoons white or red wine vinegar
2	tablespoons slivered green onion
1	teaspoon grated orange peel

1 Heat 2 tablespoons of the vegetable oil in large nonstick skillet over high heat until hot. Add ginger; sauté 30 to 60 seconds or until fragrant. Add onions; sauté 2 to 3 minutes to soften slightly. Add cabbage and soy sauce; sauté 3 to 4 minutes or until cabbage is wilted and most of moisture is evaporated. Remove from heat; stir in cilantro and sesame oil. Place in medium bowl to cool.

2 In center of each skin, place heaping teaspoonful of cabbage mixture. Moisten edges of skin with additional water. Fold skin in half to form half-moon shape. Pinch and pleat top layer of skin along rounded edge. Press edges of skin together to seal.

3 Heat 1 tablespoon of the vegetable oil in large nonstick skillet over high heat until hot. Reduce heat to medium-high; add half of the pot stickers, unfluted side down. Cook 2 to 3 minutes or until lightly browned on bottom. Add ⅓ cup of the water; cover and steam 3 to 4 minutes. Remove cover; cook an additional 1 to 2 minutes or until pot stickers are deep brown on bottom. Remove from skillet and repeat process, using remaining 1 tablespoon vegetable oil and remaining ⅓ cup water to cook second half of pot stickers.

4 For Sauce: In small bowl, combine soy sauce, orange juice, water, vinegar, green onion and grated peel. Serve immediately.

24 pot stickers.
Preparation time: 40 minutes.
Ready to serve: 52 minutes.
Per sticker: 60 calories, 4 g total fat (.5 g saturated fat), 5 mg cholesterol, 265 mg sodium, 0.5 g fiber

STUFFED BELL PEPPERS

Who doesn't love *Stuffed Bell Peppers*, a quick-and-easy dinner? So here they are for the grill — but updated a bit. They're stuffed with a wild rice salad made with pecans, cranberries and chutney. Wild rice isn't rice at all — it's a wild grass grain, native to the Upper Midwest. Buy any blend you prefer and cook it according to package directions.

6   medium green, red or yellow bell peppers
3   cups cooked wild rice, cooled
½   cup chopped pecans
½   cup mango chutney
½   cup chopped fresh cilantro
¼   cup dried cranberries or currants
2   green onions, minced
½   teaspoon salt
¾   cup (3 oz.) shredded asiago, pepper, pepper-jack or Swiss cheese

1 Heat grill for direct cooking.

2 Place peppers on gas grill directly over high heat or on charcoal grill directly over high-heat coals. Cover; grill, gently turning with metal spatula, about 6 minutes or until charred all over. (Do not use tongs — peppers cannot be pierced if they are to be stuffed.) Place peppers in large bowl; seal with plastic wrap. Set aside to steam 10 minutes.

3 Meanwhile, in medium bowl, mix wild rice, pecans, chutney, cilantro, dried cranberries, green onions and salt.

4 Peel peppers; slit each along 1 side, then gently seed. Using slit, stuff each pepper with wild rice mixture. Top each with 2 tablespoons cheese.

5 Place large sheet of aluminum foil on gas grill directly over high heat or on charcoal grill directly over high-heat coals. Place stuffed peppers on foil. Cover; grill 5 minutes or until cheese melts and stuffing is heated through.

6 servings.
Preparation time: 25 minutes.
Ready to serve: 35 minutes.
Per serving: 265 calories, 11.5 g total fat (3.5 g saturated fat), 15 mg cholesterol, 575 mg sodium, 4 g fiber.

GREEN BEANS PROVENÇALE

Herbes de Provence is a blend of dried spices common to the southern France area called Provence. The blend can vary in content, but usually contains thyme, savory, marjoram, basil and sometimes lavender. This dish can easily be doubled to serve a larger crowd at any springtime meal; use a wok instead of a skillet to rewarm the beans.

2 lb. green beans, trimmed
2 tablespoons olive oil
1 red bell pepper, cut into strips
1½ teaspoons *herbes de Provence*
¼ teaspoon salt
¼ cup pine nuts, toasted*

1 Bring 2 quarts water to a boil in large pot over high heat. Add beans; return to a boil. Cook beans until crisp-tender, about 10 minutes. Drain; run under cold water to stop cooking. (Beans may be cooked ahead. Cover and refrigerate.)

2 Heat oil in large skillet over medium-high heat until hot. Add bell pepper; sauté 1 to 2 minutes. Add beans; cook 5 minutes or until heated, stirring occasionally.

3 Sprinkle with *herbes de Provence*, salt and pine nuts; stir to coat.

8 servings.
Preparation time: 20 minutes.
Ready to serve: 35 minutes.
Per serving: 80 calories, 6 g total fat (1 g saturated fat), 0 mg cholesterol, 85 mg sodium, 3.5 g fiber.

Cooking Tip

* Toast pine nuts in batches in dry skillet. Or place pine nuts in 15x10x1-inch pan; bake at 350°F for 7 to 9 minutes or until golden brown, stirring occasionally.

SESAME ASPARAGUS

Make sure you purchase toasted, dark sesame oil for use in this dish. Used as a flavoring agent in this or any other Asian cooking, it adds a rich, nutty flavor.

1 tablespoon oyster sauce
1 tablespoon soy sauce
1 tablespoon dry sherry or white wine
1 teaspoon cornstarch
1½ teaspoons dark sesame oil
2 tablespoons sesame seeds
1 tablespoon vegetable oil
1½ teaspoons minced fresh ginger
1 teaspoon minced garlic
1 lb. asparagus, trimmed, cut diagonally into 1½-inch pieces
1 large carrot, cut diagonally into thin pieces
½ cup chicken broth
1 bunch green onions, cut diagonally into 1-inch pieces

1 In small bowl, combine oyster sauce, soy sauce and sherry. Add cornstarch; stir to dissolve. Stir in sesame oil. Set aside.

2 Place sesame seeds in unheated wok. Brown over medium heat until seeds turn golden, about 2 to 3 minutes. Remove seeds; set aside. Increase heat to high. Add oil; swirl to coat wok. Add ginger, garlic, asparagus and carrot; stir-fry 2 minutes. Add broth; cover and cook an additional 2 minutes or until asparagus and carrot are almost crisp-tender. Uncover. Add green onions; stir-fry an additional 1 minute. Add oyster sauce mixture; stir until thickened. Toss with sesame seeds.

4 servings.
Preparation time: 30 minutes.
Ready to serve: 30 minutes.
Per serving: 125 calories, 8 g total fat (1 g saturated fat), 0 mg cholesterol, 575 mg sodium, 3 g fiber.

HARD-COOKED EGG AND BACON SANDWICHES

These sandwiches make for a hearty but not heavy springtime lunch.

1 teaspoon mustard
¼ cup mayonnaise
½ teaspoon Worcestershire sauce
¼ teaspoon salt
¼ teaspoon freshly ground pepper
8 hard-cooked eggs, peeled, chilled, sliced (¼ inch)
1 cup peeled diced celery (¼ inch)
1 cup cooked diced bacon (¼ inch)
½ cup diced red onion (¼ inch)
4 lettuce leaves
8 slices whole wheat bread
2 tomatoes, sliced

1 In small bowl, combine mustard, mayonnaise, Worcestershire sauce, salt and pepper.

2 Place eggs in medium bowl; add celery, bacon and onions. Top with mustard mixture. Very gently fold together to combine. Keep egg slices as large as possible without breaking up. Salad will be on the dry side.

3 To make sandwiches, pile egg mixture on top of lettuce on whole wheat bread. Top with tomatoes and another slice of whole wheat bread. Do not cut sandwich in half, as the filling will fall out.

4 servings.
Preparation time: 15 minutes.
Ready to serve: 15 minutes.
Per serving: 530 calories, 33.5 g total fat (8.5 g saturated fat), 450 mg cholesterol, 1150 mg sodium, 5.5 g fiber.

Chef's Notes

- This mixture also makes a great dinner salad with fresh-baked sweet rolls.
- Sweet pickles are a tasty side. Or, if you wish, dice them fine and add to the filling.
- Use your imagination for extra ingredients.

PESTO CHICKEN SALAD SANDWICHES

For a warm sandwich: Heat a stovetop grill pan. Omit the lettuce. Grill prepared sandwich until it's lightly golden on both sides and the cheese has just begun to melt.

2	cups shredded cooked chicken
½	cup prepared pesto*
½	cup chopped red bell pepper
2	cups curly green leaf lettuce
8	thin slices red onion
2	oz. sliced provolone cheese
4	squares (about 6x6-inch) focaccia bread, split in half horizontally, warmed

1 In medium bowl, combine chicken and pesto. Stir in bell pepper.

2 Layer lettuce, onion and cheese on bottom half of each focaccia square. Spread each with about ½ cup chicken mixture. Top with the other half focaccia. Cut each sandwich into halves, diagonally.

4 sandwiches.
Preparation time: 15 minutes.
Ready to serve: 15 minutes.
Per serving: 910 calories, 45 g total fat (10 g saturated fat), 75 mg cholesterol, 1790 mg sodium, 5 g fiber.

Variations

Any leftover grilled, roasted or sautéed chicken is delicious when used in salads. But for the most tender and moist chicken of all, choose poached chicken. Here's how to poach:

- **Chicken Breasts.** Place boneless skinless chicken breasts in a skillet. Add cold water to cover. Cover skillet and bring to a boil over medium heat. Reduce heat to low; simmer 10 minutes or until chicken juices run clear and internal temperature reaches 175°F to 180°F. Let cool. Shred chicken.

- **Bone-in Breasts.** Simmer chicken 15 to 20 minutes or until chicken juices run clear and internal temperature reaches 175°F to 180°F. Let cool. Remove skin. Shred chicken.

- **Whole Chicken (about 3½ lb.).** Place chicken in a large pot. Add a handful of parsley, a bay leaf and 1 rib of celery. Add water to cover. Bring to a boil over medium-high heat. Reduce heat to low. Simmer 25 to 30 minutes or until chicken juices run clear and internal temperature reaches 175°F to 180°F. Let cool. Remove skin. Shred chicken.

Cooking Tip

* Some prepared pesto is drier than others. If the chicken mixture appears dry, stir in about 1 tablespoon olive oil.

LACED SPINACH-RICOTTA BREAD

Stromboli, calzone, pasties or meat pies. Whatever the name, these savory filled breads and pastries make great portable lunches or snacks. The bread machine short-cuts the dough-making process, and the filling variations are endless. Lacing the dough over the spinach and cheese makes the bread look more interesting and is no more difficult than just folding the dough over a filling.

3 cups unbleached bread flour
1 cup lukewarm water
2 tablespoons olive oil
1 (¼-oz.) pkg. active dry yeast or 2¼ teaspoons bread machine yeast
6 garlic cloves, minced
½ teaspoon salt
1 (10-oz.) pkg. frozen chopped spinach, thawed, squeezed dry
1 cup low-fat ricotta cheese
2 egg yolks
½ cup (2 oz.) freshly grated Parmesan cheese
¼ teaspoon freshly grated nutmeg
  Cornmeal
1 cup (4 oz.) shredded smoked provolone
1 egg, beaten

1 Place flour, water, oil, yeast, garlic and salt into 1½-lb. loaf bread machine, following manufacturer's instructions. Select Dough cycle; press Start.

2 Prepare filling: In medium bowl, mix spinach, ricotta, egg yolks, Parmesan cheese and nutmeg. Turn dough out of bread pan onto floured surface. Knead 30 seconds until smooth; cover and let rest 10 minutes. Sprinkle large baking sheet with cornmeal.

3 Roll dough into 15x10-inch rectangle. Spread filling lengthwise over center third of dough. Sprinkle provolone over filling. With sharp knife, make cuts from filling to edges of dough at 1-inch intervals along sides. Alternating sides, fold strips at an angle across filling. Use foil or parchment paper to transfer filled dough to baking sheet. Cover; let rise in warm place 45 minutes or until nearly doubled in size.

4 Heat oven to 350°F. Brush dough with beaten egg; bake 35 minutes or until golden brown. Cool slightly before slicing.

16 servings.
Preparation time: 3 hours, 15 minutes.
Ready to serve: 3 hours, 55 minutes.
Per serving: 190 calories, 7 g total fat (3 g saturated fat), 50 mg cholesterol, 235 mg sodium, 1 g fiber.

Variation

- **Ham and Cheese Dijon Sandwich**
  Add 3 tablespoons Dijon mustard to dough. Prepare dough and roll out as directed. Layer 1 cup chopped smoked ham and ½ cup cubed Swiss cheese down center of dough. Lace up as directed.

RISO AND PEA SOUP

Risi e bisi is a classic dish of Venice, served in the spring to honor St. Mark. This version uses pasta instead of rice, and the main reason to make it is because there's a harvest of fresh spring peas in the garden but no rice in the pantry. This version is not as creamy as the one made with rice because pasta does not break down in the same way as the grain. But it's a very good soup, best made with young peas.

1	tablespoon kosher (coarse) salt plus more to taste
6	oz. riso (seed-shaped pasta)
4	tablespoons unsalted butter
1	shallot, minced
1½	cups freshly shelled peas
3	cups chicken stock
10	fresh mint leaves
1	tablespoon minced fresh Italian parsley
1	tablespoon minced fresh chives
⅛	teaspoon freshly ground pepper
½	cup (2 oz.) grated Pecorino cheese

1 Fill large pot two-thirds full of water; add 1 tablespoon salt. Bring to a boil over high heat. Cook riso according to package directions; drain. Set aside.

2 Meanwhile, melt 2 tablespoons of the butter in medium skillet over medium-low heat. Add shallot; cook about 4 minutes or until soft and fragrant. Add peas and sauté an additional 4 minutes, stirring constantly. Add chicken stock; increase heat to medium-high. Bring stock to a boil; reduce heat to medium-low. Simmer about 4 minutes or until peas are almost tender. Stir cooked pasta into stock; simmer an additional 5 minutes.

3 Stack mint leaves on work surface. Using very sharp knife, cut into very thin crosswise strips. Stir mint, parsley and chives into stock; season with salt and pepper. Remove from heat; stir cheese into soup. Ladle into warm bowls. Divide remaining 2 tablespoons butter among servings and use tip of spoon to swirl — not mix — butter into soup.

4 servings.
Preparation time: 20 minutes.
Ready to serve: 40 minutes.
Per serving: 395 calories, 17 g total fat (10 g saturated fat), 40 mg cholesterol, 1230 mg sodium, 5 g fiber.

FRUITED CABERNET BISQUE

Here's a cool, spring soup with pureed seasonal fruits. Substitute fruits as desired.

Strawberries, blueberries and papaya may be used, depending on availability and taste.

1	large ripe mango
3	large apricots
2	large ripe peaches
2	black plums
3	tablespoons honey
½	cup cabernet wine
2	cups apricot juice*
8 to 10	mint leaves
1½	tablespoons fresh lime juice
	Whipped cream

1 Remove seeds from mango, apricots, peaches and plums. Cut into thin wedges. Set aside.

2 In medium pan, warm honey over medium-high heat. Sauté prepared fruits 2 to 3 minutes.

3 Stir in wine and juice. Reduce heat to medium. Simmer 10 minutes or until fruit is soft.

4 Cool slightly before pouring into blender. Add mint leaves and lime juice; blend until smooth.

5 Serve chilled or at room temperature. Garnish with drizzle of softly whipped cream.

4 servings.
Preparation time: 15 minutes.
Ready to serve: 1 hour, 30 minutes.
Per serving: 170 calories, 0 g fat (0 g saturated fat), 0 mg cholesterol, 6 mg sodium, 4.5 g fiber.

Cooking Tip
* If soup is too thick, add a little extra apricot juice bit by bit.

WARM TAGLIATELLE SALAD WITH GRILLED FIGS, PROSCIUTTO, ARUGULA AND BLACK PEPPER

Add three-quarters of a teaspoon of freshly ground pepper to the pasta flour. It will add an appealing jolt of heat — a sultry sort of bass note — to this dish.

1 tablespoon plus ¼ teaspoon kosher (coarse) salt
6 black figs, cut in half lengthwise
4 tablespoons extra-virgin olive oil
⅓ cup semolina flour
⅔ cup unbleached all-purpose flour
1 egg, room temperature
2 teaspoons water
3 oz. prosciutto, ⅛ inch thick, cut into ½-inch crosswise strips
2 tablespoons balsamic vinegar
⅛ teaspoon freshly ground pepper
3 cups young arugula

1 Heat grill. Bring 2 quarts water to a boil; add 1 tablespoon of the salt.

2 Meanwhile, use pastry brush to coat cut surfaces of figs with 1 tablespoon of the olive oil. Place figs, cut side down, on gas grill over medium heat or on charcoal grill 4 to 6 inches from medium coals. Cook 5 to 7 minutes or until hot. Transfer to plate.

3 Combine flours and remaining ¼ teaspoon salt in food processor; pulse 3 or 4 times. With machine running, add egg and water. Continue processing 45 seconds or until dough forms soft ball, stopping to scrape bowl with rubber spatula. Sprinkle flour on clean work surface. Knead dough 2 to 3 times. Break dough into 3 equal pieces. Pat dough into rectangle; flatten dough with palm to ⅜-inch thickness. Set pasta machine on widest setting; crank dough through machine 10 to 12 times, dusting with flour and folding in half after each pass (dough will become a lighter color and will begin to feel smooth and elastic).

4 Cook pasta in boiling water about 2 minutes or until just done; drain. Rinse thoroughly in cool water and drain. Transfer pasta to medium bowl; add prosciutto. Drizzle with 1½ tablespoons olive oil and 1 tablespoon of the balsamic vinegar. Season with salt and pepper. Set aside.

5 Place arugula in large bowl. Season with salt; toss. Drizzle with remaining 1½ tablespoons of the olive oil and remaining 1 tablespoon balsamic vinegar; toss again. Divide arugula evenly among salad plates. Top each portion with 1 cup pasta and prosciutto. Divide grilled figs among plates; season with pepper.

4 servings.
Preparation time: 45 minutes.
Ready to serve: 55 minutes.
Per serving: 365 calories, 18 g total fat (4 g saturated fat), 65 mg cholesterol, 900 mg sodium, 4 g fiber.

MEDITERRANEAN COUSCOUS SALAD

Couscous looks like grain, but it's pasta made from semolina flour. Pita bread, cut into wedges and crisped in the oven, makes the perfect accompaniment to this wonderful springtime salad.

1   tablespoon kosher (coarse) salt
2   cups Israeli (large) couscous
1   (3-inch) cinnamon stick
1   tablespoon cumin seeds
1   tablespoon coriander seeds
¼   cup extra-virgin olive oil
1   tablespoon fresh lemon juice
½   teaspoon salt
¼   teaspoon freshly ground pepper
1   lemon, rinsed, chopped
½   cup fresh mint, chopped
½   cup grated carrot
¼   cup chopped green onions

1 Fill large pot two-thirds full of water; add kosher salt. Bring to a boil over high heat. Add couscous; cook 10 minutes or until *al dente*. Drain. Rinse thoroughly in cool water; drain. Transfer to large bowl.

2 In skillet, toast cinnamon stick, cumin seeds and coriander seeds over medium heat until fragrant. Remove from heat; let cool. Grind spices using mortar and pestle or coffee grinder reserved for spices.

3 In small bowl or pitcher, combine spices, olive oil, lemon juice, ½ teaspoon salt and pepper. Add to couscous; toss well. Add lemon, mint, carrot and green onions; toss again.

6 (1-cup) servings.
Preparation time: 15 minutes.
Ready to serve: 25 minutes.
Per serving: 265 calories, 10.5 g total fat (1.5 g saturated fat), 0 mg cholesterol, 630 mg sodium, 2.5 g fiber.

ASPARAGUS WITH SWEET RED PEPPER DRESSING

In Europe, everything seems to come to a halt when late spring's first asparagus arrives in the market. It's the time to sit down with a giant platter of thick stems and eat them with your fingers. The thickest stems are the tastiest. Be sure to choose those without any woodiness showing at the stem end. They should be green from top to bottom.

2	roasted red bell peppers
2	garlic cloves, chopped
2	tablespoons fresh oregano
2	teaspoons fresh lemon juice
½	teaspoon salt
⅓	cup olive oil
1	lb. fresh asparagus
½	cup (2 oz.) crumbled soft goat cheese

1 In blender, combine bell peppers, garlic, oregano, lemon juice and salt. Cover; blend until smooth. With blender running, add olive oil in a steady stream. (Pepper puree can be prepared up to 24 hours ahead. Cover and refrigerate; bring to room temperature before serving.)

2 Break tough ends from asparagus. Using vegetable peeler, peel asparagus from just below flowering top to the end.

3 Fill skillet with water. Bring to a boil over high heat; add asparagus. Cook 5 minutes or until tender. Drain; run asparagus under cold water to stop cooking.

4 Arrange asparagus on platter or divide among 4 plates. Drizzle each serving with about ¼ cup dressing; sprinkle with goat cheese.

4 servings.
Preparation time: 15 minutes.
Ready to serve: 25 minutes.
Per serving: 240 calories, 20 g total fat (4.5 g saturated fat), 10 mg cholesterol, 345 mg sodium, 2.5 g fiber.

ARTICHOKE, CHICKEN AND PASTA SALAD

Fresh artichokes in spring have a nutty, earthy flavor and texture — something quite different from those you find in a can or jar, which taste primarily of the brine or vinegar in which they are preserved.

1	tablespoon kosher (coarse) salt plus more to taste
8	oz. capanelle (flower-shaped pasta)
1	shallot, minced
2½	tablespoons fresh lemon juice
⅛	teaspoon freshly ground pepper
2	teaspoons minced fresh tarragon or 1 teaspoon dried beaux herbs
¼	cup extra-virgin olive oil
2	fresh artichoke hearts, cooked, thinly sliced
½	cup cracked green olives, pitted, sliced
1	cup cooked shredded dark chicken meat

1 Fill large pot two-thirds full of water; add 1 tablespoon salt. Bring to a boil over high heat. Cook capanelle according to package directions; drain. Rinse and drain thoroughly in cool water. Transfer pasta to shallow bowl.

2 Meanwhile, in small bowl, cover shallot with lemon juice. Season with salt, pepper and 2 teaspoons tarragon; whisk in olive oil.

3 Add artichoke hearts, olives and chicken to cooked pasta. Pour dressing over pasta and vegetables; toss gently but thoroughly.

4 servings.
Preparation time: 15 minutes.
Ready to serve: 30 minutes.
Per serving: 490 calories, 26 g total fat (4 g saturated fat), 30 mg cholesterol, 1010 mg sodium, 4 g fiber.

PAPARDELLE WITH PROSCIUTTO, SPINACH AND CREAM

Spinach — often available as a spingtime green — is best cooked very quickly so that it retains its fresh flavors. Papardelle, a very broad noodle, is usually sold in half-pound packages, enough for a main course for two or three adults, or a first course for three or four people.

1 tablespoon kosher (coarse) salt plus more to taste
1 (8.8-oz.) pkg. papardelle
1¼ cups whipping cream
1 teaspoon freshly ground nutmeg plus more to taste
⅛ teaspoon freshly ground pepper
3 oz. prosciutto, sliced ¹⁄₁₆-inch thick
8 oz. young spinach leaves, washed
½ cup (2 oz.) grated fresh asiago cheese

1 Fill large pot two-thirds full of water; add 1 tablespoon salt. Bring to a boil over high heat. Cook papardelle according to package directions; drain. Do not rinse.

2 Meanwhile, pour cream into medium saucepan; bring to a boil over medium heat. Stir often. Reduce heat to medium-low; simmer about 10 minutes or until reduced by one-third. Add nutmeg and season with pepper; set aside and keep hot. Cut prosciutto into thin crosswise strips; heat through in medium skillet over medium heat. Add spinach; cover and cook about 2 minutes or until spinach is just wilted. Stir spinach and prosciutto into hot cream.

3 Transfer pasta to shallow bowl; sprinkle cheese over pasta. Pour cream mixture over cheese; toss gently but thoroughly. Season with additional salt, nutmeg and pepper. Divide pasta evenly among plates.

4 servings.
Preparation time: 15 minutes.
Ready to serve: 20 minutes.
Per serving: 765 calories, 40 g total fat (24 g saturated fat), 140 mg cholesterol, 1180 mg sodium, 4.5 g fiber.

Little Ropes with Rib-Eye Steak, Grilled Onions and Gorgonzola Butter

The gorgonzola butter will keep, wrapped tightly and stored in the refrigerator, for one week.

Toss leftover butter with steamed green beans or hot pasta to accent another spring meal.

1	tablespoon kosher (coarse) salt plus more to taste
8 to 10	oz. pasta al ceppo, gemelli or strozzapreti
½	cup unsalted butter, softened
¾	cup (3 oz.) Italian gorgonzola cheese
2	teaspoons minced fresh rosemary
2	teaspoons freshly ground pepper plus more to taste
1	red onion, peeled
2	teaspoons olive oil
2	beef rib-eye steaks, 1½ inches thick
4	small rosemary sprigs

1 Heat grill. Fill large pot two-thirds full of water; add 1 tablespoon of the salt. Bring to a boil over high heat. Cook al ceppo according to package directions; drain. Do not rinse.

2 Meanwhile, in food processor, combine butter, gorgonzola, rosemary and 2 teaspoons of the pepper; pulse about 15 seconds or until mixture comes together. Scrape sides with rubber spatula; pulse again. Transfer mixture to sheet of plastic wrap; wrap butter loosely and roll into log about 1¼ inches in diameter. Wrap tightly; place in freezer while preparing onion and steaks.

3 Cut onion in half crosswise; rub with olive oil. Place on gas grill over medium-high heat or on charcoal grill 4 to 6 inches from medium-high coals. Grill onion, turning occasionally, 15 to 20 minutes or until tender; set aside.

4 Season steaks on both sides with salt and pepper. Grill steaks 3 minutes; turn. Cook an additional 3 minutes; turn again, rotating direction to mark steaks. For rare steaks, cook about 2 minutes; turn and cook an additional 2 minutes. Remove from grill; cover with aluminum foil and let stand 5 minutes.

5 Cut grilled onion into thin horizontal strips. Place cooked pasta and onion strips in medium bowl; cut several rounds of gorgonzola butter and toss with pasta until butter is melted. Cut steaks into ¼-inch-thick diagonal strips; add to pasta. Season with salt and pepper; toss quickly. Divide pasta evenly among serving plates; garnish each portion with rosemary sprig.

4 servings.
Preparation time: 20 minutes.
Ready to serve: 30 minutes.
Per serving: 1120 calories, 75 g total fat (35 g saturated fat), 240 mg cholesterol, 950 mg sodium, 3 g fiber.

CHICKEN BREASTS WITH APRICOT-PISTACHIO STUFFING

Pretzels form the base of this bold stuffing. Bake separately in a baking dish or well-greased individual muffin pans. Or tuck pretzel stuffing under the chicken breasts. The stuffing may be made in advance and refrigerated, but to avoid contamination, do not place under chicken until just before cooking. The classic mixture of *fines herbes* includes chervil, chives, parsley and tarragon, and is available in most markets.

Stuffing
1½ cups crushed pretzels
2 ribs celery, cut into 2-inch pieces
10 dried apricot halves
¼ cup shelled pistachios
1½ teaspoons dried *fines herbes*
¼ cup plus 4 teaspoons margarine, melted
2 tablespoons water

Chicken
4 (8-oz.) chicken breasts
Dash paprika

1 Heat oven to 350°F.

2 Spray 8-inch square pan with nonstick cooking spray.

3 In food processor, chop pretzels, celery, apricots and pistachios until coarse bread crumbs form. Add *fines herbes*, 3 tablespoons of the margarine and water; process to mix.

4 Place ¼ cup of the mixture into pan. Arrange one chicken breast on top; press lightly. Repeat with remaining stuffing and chicken breasts. Bake any extra stuffing separately.

5 Slip 1 teaspoon of the margarine under skin of each chicken breast. Brush chicken with remaining margarine. Sprinkle lightly with paprika.

6 Bake 1 hour or until internal temperature reaches 180°F.

4 servings.
Preparation time: 25 minutes.
Ready to serve: 1 hour, 30 minutes.
Per serving: 540 calories, 31.5 g fat (6 g saturated fat), 97 mg cholesterol, 565 mg sodium, 3.5 g fiber.

Chef's Note
- For individual servings, fill 4 to 6 well-greased mini soufflé dishes about ¾ full. Drizzle with a little oil or melted margarine and bake the last 15 to 20 minutes of cooking time until nicely browned. Or spoon into a well-greased 1-quart dish and bake at 350°F for 30 minutes or until crusty on top.

BLACK BEAN, CORN AND BELL PEPPER TART

The cornmeal crust is a take-off on a Mexican tamale filling. To make this colorful dish even spicier, leave the seeds in the jalapeño before chopping. Something hot for spring!

Crust

1½	teaspoons chili powder
1	teaspoon baking powder
1	teaspoon cumin
¾	teaspoon salt
2	tablespoons vegetable oil
1¼	cups cornmeal
1	cup boiling water
1	egg

Filling

1	(15-oz.) can black beans, rinsed, drained
1½	cups cooked corn
1	red bell pepper, diced
½	cup chopped green onions
½	cup coarsely chopped cilantro
1	large jalapeño pepper, seeded, minced
¼	teaspoon salt
⅛	teaspoon freshly ground pepper
1½	cups (6 oz.) shredded cheddar and mozzarella cheese blend

Garnish

1	cup salsa

1 Heat oven to 400°F. Grease 10-inch springform pan or pie plate with nonstick cooking spray.

2 In medium bowl, combine chili powder, baking powder, cumin and salt; mix well. Stir in oil. Mix in cornmeal until evenly coated. Stir in water; let sit several minutes. Beat in egg.

3 Press cornmeal mixture over bottom and ½ inch up sides of springform pan.

4 In another medium bowl, combine black beans, corn, bell pepper, onions, cilantro, jalapeño pepper, salt, pepper and 1 cup of the cheese; mix well. Spoon into crust, pressing down slightly. Sprinkle with remaining ½ cup cheese. Bake 30 minutes or until heated through and cheese is melted. Remove sides of springform pan. Serve with salsa.

6 servings.
Preparation time: 20 minutes.
Ready to serve: 50 minutes.
Per serving: 380 calories, 14 g total fat (5.5 g saturated fat), 60 mg cholesterol, 880 mg sodium, 8 g fiber.

PENNE WITH ASPARAGUS AND TOASTED HAZELNUTS

Once you eat roasted asparagus, you'll never again return to boiling or steaming it.

Roasting intensifies the flavors of this classic spring vegetable and, as an added bonus,

eliminates the need to peel it — even the larger spears.

2 tablespoons olive oil
1 lb. asparagus spears, tough ends removed, cut into 2-inch lengths
1 tablespoon kosher (coarse) salt plus more to taste
⅛ teaspoon freshly ground pepper
12 oz. trenne or penne (tube-shaped pasta)
2 tablespoons clarified butter (see Chef's Note)
1 cup (4 oz.) shredded or grated smoked mozzarella
½ cup shelled hazelnuts, toasted, skinned, coarsely chopped

1 Heat oven to 450°F. In large bowl, toss olive oil with asparagus until evenly coated. Arrange asparagus on 15x10-inch baking sheet in single layer; season with salt and pepper. Bake 7 to 10 minutes or until just tender. Remove from oven and let cool until easy to handle.

2 Fill large pot two-thirds full of water; add 1 tablespoon salt. Bring to a boil over high heat. Cook trenne according to package directions; drain. Do not rinse. Transfer cooked pasta to serving bowl.

3 Meanwhile, cut each piece of roasted asparagus in half lengthwise. Melt clarified butter in medium skillet over medium heat; add asparagus. Toss and cook until heated through. Pour cooked asparagus over pasta; add mozzarella. Toss gently but thoroughly. Divide pasta evenly among plates; top each portion with hazelnuts.

4 servings.
Preparation time: 20 minutes.
Ready to serve: 30 minutes.
Per serving: 635 calories, 29 g total fat (10 g saturated fat), 40 mg cholesterol, 775 mg sodium, 5 g fiber.

Chef's Note
- To make clarified butter, melt 1 cup of butter over medium heat in medium saucepan. Skim and discard foam from top of melted butter. Carefully pour melted butter into small container, being careful to leave milk solids in bottom of pan.

ACINI DI PEPE WITH PORTOBELLOS, FAVAS AND ASIAGO

There's something about the way this little round pasta, named for peppercorns, teases the palate. It is so delightful and compelling that you don't want to quit eating it. If you don't have fresh favas, use fresh spring peas or omit them entirely.

1	tablespoon kosher (coarse) salt plus more to taste
8	oz. acini di pepe (peppercorn-shaped pasta)
2	tablespoons olive oil
2	oz. pancetta, diced
1	red onion, diced
2	portobello mushrooms, trimmed, diced
¾	cup dry white wine
⅛	teaspoon freshly ground pepper
¾	cup shelled fava beans (from 1 lb. of beans in pods), blanched, peeled
1	cup (4 oz.) grated aged Italian asiago cheese

1 Fill large pot two-thirds full of water; add 1 tablespoon salt. Bring to a boil over high heat. Cook acini di pepe according to package directions; drain. Rinse and drain thoroughly in cool water. Transfer cooked pasta to medium bowl. Drizzle with 1 tablespoon of the olive oil; toss to coat thoroughly.

2 Heat oven to 350°F. Heat remaining 1 tablespoon olive oil in medium skillet over medium heat until hot. Cook pancetta about 5 minutes or until translucent. Add onion; sauté 5 minutes. Add mushrooms; sauté until soft, stirring frequently.

3 Add wine; toss mixture. Simmer until wine is nearly evaporated, about 10 minutes. Season with salt and pepper. Add pancetta mixture and favas to pasta bowl; toss gently but thoroughly. Stir in ½ cup of the cheese; pour mixture into shallow baking dish. Sprinkle remaining ½ cup cheese over pasta; bake about 15 minutes or until cheese is melted and just turning golden brown. Remove from oven; let stand 5 minutes before serving.

4 servings.
Preparation time: 30 minutes.
Ready to serve: 1 hour.
Per serving: 585 calories, 29 g total fat (11 g saturated fat), 35 mg cholesterol, 1125 mg sodium, 5 g fiber.

SCALOPPINI

The best meat to use is from the loin or the tenderloins themselves. You can also use turkey tenderloins for an extra-light spring touch.

8   (3-oz.) slices veal or pork
½   cup seasoned flour (see Chef's Note)
2   teaspoons minced fresh parsley
1   teaspoon grated lemon peel
½   teaspoon freshly ground pepper
2   tablespoons clarified butter (see page 42)
2   tablespoons finely diced shallots
1   garlic clove, finely minced
½   cup dry white wine
2   teaspoons minced fresh tarragon

1 Dredge veal slices in seasoned flour; shaking off excess. Set aside.

2 In large bowl, combine parsley, lemon peel and pepper.

3 In large skillet, melt butter over medium heat. Add shallots, garlic and veal slices; sauté until veal is browned, about 2 minutes. Turn, stir shallots and brown opposite side; add wine and tarragon. Simmer 2 minutes.

4 Transfer veal to heated serving platter. Sprinkle with parsley mixture. Top with sauce from pan. Serve with pasta, egg noodles or spätzles, if desired.

4 servings.
Preparation time: 10 minutes.
Ready to serve: 25 minutes.
Per serving: 175 calories, 6 g total fat (3.5 g saturated fat), 70 mg cholesterol, 450 mg sodium, 1 g fiber.

Chef's Note

- To make seasoned flour, combine 1 cup all-purpose flour, 2 teaspoons salt and ⅛ teaspoon ground white pepper in small bowl; mix well.

SPRING FRUIT CRISP

If you feel adventurous, try some other fruits in this great crisp. But to start, the rhubarb and strawberries are wonderful. The topping for any fruit crisp is a streusel topping. Use the basic Streusel Mix (page 46) or this richer version below.

Crisp
2	cups diced rhubarb
2	cups strawberries, hulled
1	cup sugar
2	tablespoons all-purpose flour
⅛	teaspoon ground cloves

Topping
1	cup packed brown sugar
¾	cup all-purpose flour
½	teaspoon cinnamon
	Dash ground cloves
6	tablespoons butter, chilled
½	cup chopped pecans

1 Heat oven to 350°F. Spray 9-inch square pan with nonstick cooking spray.

2 In large bowl, toss rhubarb and strawberries with sugar, flour and cloves. Pour into pan. Set aside.

3 In small bowl, mix brown sugar, flour, cinnamon and cloves. Cut in butter with pastry blender or fingers until mixture crumbles. Stir in pecans.

4 Spread nut mixture over rhubarb and strawberries.

5 Bake 45 minutes or until golden brown and bubbly.

8 servings.
Preparation time: 20 minutes.
Ready to serve: 1 hour, 5 minutes.
Per serving: 390 calories, 14 g fat (6 g saturated fat), 25 mg cholesterol, 70 mg sodium, 2.5 g fiber.

Chef's Notes

- Mature rhubarb, with its thick, red sour stalks, is a member of the buckwheat family. Although it's usually eaten as a fruit, botanically it is a vegetable. The big, flat green leaves contain oxalic acid, which is toxic. Leaves should be removed and discarded before cooking. The stalks of rhubarb grown in hothouses are pale pink with much less flavor and tartness than the field-grown variety. In some areas, hothouse rhubarb is available year-round. Field-grown is available in late spring and early summer.

- In Britain, the traditional flavoring for rhubarb jams and desserts is ground ginger, which may be used instead of cloves in this recipe.

EASTER BABKA

Babka (or babke) are yeast-batter coffee cakes from Russia, perfect for holiday mornings spent with family and friends. Babka also makes a great, light dessert after a luncheon or dinner. The light, slightly crumbly texture is created by allowing the sponge and batter to rise before baking.

Cake
1   (¼-oz.) pkg. active dry yeast
¾   cup sugar
1   cup warm milk (105°F to 115°F)
¼   teaspoon salt
3¾ cups unbleached all-purpose flour
½   cup butter
3   eggs, slightly beaten
½   cup dark or golden raisins
1   tablespoon grated lemon peel

Streusel
¼   cup packed brown sugar
2   tablespoons unbleached all-purpose flour
¾   teaspoon ground ginger
¼   cup chopped walnuts
1   tablespoon melted butter

Topping
2   tablespoons melted butter
¼   cup apricot preserves, warmed

Baker's Note
- Yeasted coffee cakes can be baked in a variety of pans or molds. If you have decorative cake pans or Bundt cake molds, consider using them for special occasion baking. For a Bundt-style pan, sprinkle streusel in the bottom of the pan before pouring in batter. Unmold the coffee cake after baking, inverting it onto a serving plate.

1 In medium bowl, dissolve yeast and 1 teaspoon of the sugar in milk; let stand 5 minutes. Stir in salt and 1 cup of the flour; beat well. Cover; let sponge rise in warm place 1 hour or until nearly bubbly and risen.

2 In large bowl, beat remaining sugar and ½ cup butter until creamy. Beat in eggs and sponge mixture until smooth. Stir in raisins, lemon peel and remaining 2¾ cups flour; mix until smooth, thick batter forms. Cover; let rise 1 hour or until doubled in size.

3 Grease 10-inch tube pan with removable bottom. Scrape batter into pan. Cover; let rise 30 to 45 minutes or until doubled in size.

4 Meanwhile, prepare Streusel: Mix brown sugar, flour, ginger, walnuts and melted butter until crumbly.

5 Heat oven to 350°F. For Topping: Brush cake with 2 tablespoons melted butter; sprinkle with streusel. Bake 35 to 40 minutes or until light golden brown. Remove from pan; cool on wire rack. Drizzle with warm preserves.

16 servings.
Preparation time: 3 hours, 15 minutes.
Ready to serve: 4 hours, 20 minutes.
Per serving: 295 calories, 10.5 g total fat (5.5 g saturated fat), 60 mg cholesterol, 115 mg sodium, 1.5 g fiber.

HONEY-LAVENDER PLUM GRATIN

Infuse lavender blossoms into milk for a delicate perfume. This honey-sweetened, lavender-scented custard marries well with plums. A quick pass under the broiler to caramelize the top creates a simple, elegant dessert. Note that because the custard is stabilized with cornstarch, you can let it reach a gentle simmer.

Custard*

- ¾ cup reduced-fat milk
- ¾ teaspoon unsprayed fresh lavender blossoms or ¼ teaspoon dried
- 2 egg yolks
- 2 tablespoons honey
- 1 teaspoon cornstarch
- ½ teaspoon vanilla**

Fruit and Topping

- 4 medium plums, quartered, pitted
- 2 tablespoons sugar

Cooking Tips

* You can also use the custard as a sauce for fresh raspberries or figs.

** If vanilla bean is available, this is a great opportunity to use it. Replace the vanilla extract with a 3-inch piece of vanilla bean. Make a lengthwise slit in the bean with tip of sharp knife, scrape out the seeds and drop the whole bean into milk along with the lavender in step 1; let steep.

1 In small saucepan, heat milk over medium heat until steaming. Remove from heat. Add lavender; cover and steep 30 minutes.

2 Pass milk through fine sieve into medium bowl. Return strained milk to saucepan; reheat until steaming.

3 In medium bowl, whisk egg yolks, honey and cornstarch until smooth. Gradually add hot milk, whisking until blended. Return mixture to saucepan over medium heat. Cook 1½ to 2 minutes or until slightly thickened and starting to bubble gently, whisking constantly. Transfer to clean medium bowl; whisk in vanilla. Cover loosely; refrigerate at least 1 hour or until chilled. (Custard can be made ahead. Cover and refrigerate up to 2 days.)

4 Heat broiler. Spray 11x7-inch oval gratin dish or 4 individual gratin dishes with cooking spray. Spoon custard evenly over bottom of gratin dishes. Arrange plums, skin side down, in single layer over custard. Sprinkle sugar evenly over plums. Broil 5 to 7 minutes or until plums are lightly caramelized. Serve immediately.

4 servings.
Preparation time: 25 minutes.
Ready to serve: 2 hours, 15 minutes.
Per serving: 150 calories, 4 g total fat (1.5 g saturated fat), 110 mg cholesterol, 25 mg sodium, 1 g fiber.

AUNT HANNI'S BLUEBERRY TORTE

What could be better than a crispy, crusty, light and fruity torte to finish off a spring meal? This could easily become one of your all-time favorite desserts. It's not hard to make, either. Fresh blueberries are best, but with a little lemon juice added, frozen berries taste just as delicious.

Crust

½ cup butter, softened
¼ cup sugar
1 egg, beaten
1½ cups all-purpose flour

Filling

¾ cup sugar
3 tablespoons cornstarch
⅛ teaspoon salt
1 cup water
1 quart fresh or frozen blueberries, thawed
2 teaspoons grated fresh ginger

Garnish

Whipped topping

Chef's Notes

- Weighting down an empty pie crust to prevent the pastry from rising during baking is called baking "blind." Cover the bottom with aluminum foil or parchment paper and cover that with dried beans or uncooked rice.
- When baking is completed, cool beans and store in a jar in a dry place. The beans may be used over and over again as pie weights.

1 Heat oven to 350°F. Spray 10-inch springform pan with nonstick cooking spray.

2 For Crust: Cut butter into 6 or 8 pieces. Place in food processor with sugar, egg and ½ cup of the flour. Pulse 2 or 3 times to mix. Pulse, adding remaining 1 cup flour to form ball. Press dough into bottom of pan and 1 inch up sides; prick all over with fork.

3 To keep bottom of pastry shell from rising during baking, cover pastry with sheet of aluminum foil weighted down with 2 cups of dried beans or rice. Bake 15 minutes or until edges just begin to brown. Remove dried beans and foil. Cool on wire rack.

4 For Filling: Combine sugar, cornstarch, salt and water in large saucepan. Bring to a boil over medium-high heat, stirring constantly. Cook 1 minute. Remove from heat; gently stir in blueberries and ginger. Cool before pouring into baked shell. Garnish with rosettes of whipped cream.

8 servings.
Preparation time: 25 minutes.
Ready to serve: 55 minutes.
Per serving: 275 calories, 10 g fat (6 g saturated fat), 46 mg cholesterol, 100 mg sodium, 2 g fiber.

STRAWBERRY SHORTCAKES WITH LEMON VERBENA CREAM

Here is a lightened-up version of classic strawberry shortcake. Instead of straight whipped cream, the topping is made from vanilla yogurt and just enough real whipped cream to lighten the texture and contribute a luxurious taste.

Lemon Verbena Cream
1½ cups low-fat vanilla yogurt
½ cup whipping cream
4 teaspoons very finely chopped fresh lemon verbena

Shortcakes
2 cups all-purpose flour
2 tablespoons plus 2 teaspoons sugar
1 tablespoon baking powder
½ teaspoon baking soda
½ teaspoon salt
6 tablespoons butter, cut into small pieces
1 cup buttermilk
2 teaspoons reduced-fat milk

Strawberry Filling
6 cups (1½ lb.) strawberries, hulled, sliced
2 tablespoons sugar

Garnish
Fresh lemon verbena sprigs

1 Line sieve or colander with cheesecloth; set over medium bowl at least ½ inch from bottom. Spoon yogurt into sieve. Cover; drain in refrigerator 1½ hours. Meanwhile, place small bowl and beaters in freezer to chill. In chilled bowl with chilled beaters, whip cream to soft peaks. Push to one side of bowl. Discard whey that has drained from yogurt. Add drained yogurt and lemon verbena to whipped cream. With rubber spatula, fold gently to mix. (Cream can be made ahead. Cover and refrigerate up to 8 hours.)

2 Heat oven to 425°F. Spray baking sheet with cooking spray.

3 In large bowl, combine flour, 2 tablespoons sugar, baking powder, baking soda and salt; whisk to blend. Using pastry blender or fingertips, cut in butter until mixture crumbles. Make a well in center of flour mixture; add buttermilk, stirring with fork, just until dough clumps together. Turn out onto lightly floured surface; knead several times. Roll or pat dough ¾ inch thick. Using a 3- or 3½-inch round cutter, cut out circles. Arrange shortcakes 1 inch apart on baking sheet. Gather scraps; reroll. Brush tops with milk; sprinkle with remaining 2 teaspoons sugar.

4 Bake shortcakes 15 to 20 minutes or until golden brown. Transfer to wire rack; cool at least 10 minutes. Meanwhile, in medium bowl, combine strawberries and 2 tablespoons sugar; toss gently to coat. Let stand about 20 minutes or until strawberries give off juice.

5 Just before serving, assemble shortcakes: Using serrated knife, split 6 shortcakes horizontally. Place shortcake bottoms on individual plates. Spoon about ⅓ cup strawberries and juice over each shortcake bottom. Top each with scant ¼ cup lemon verbena cream. Replace shortcake tops. Place dollop of the remaining cream on each shortcake. Spoon remaining strawberries and juice over top. Garnish with lemon verbena sprigs.

6 servings.
Preparation time: 50 minutes.
Ready to serve: 2 hours, 30 minutes.
Per serving: 455 calories, 20 g total fat (12 g saturated fat), 60 mg cholesterol, 700 mg sodium, 3 g fiber.

S P R I N G

CRAFTS

Spring means new. There's new life outside in the form of green grass, fresh flowers, warm breezes, and open windows to let it all in ... and new energy inside of you. Put that creative power to good use on these lovely craft projects for spring! With lively colors, beautiful flowers, colorful motifs and fun themes, these craft concepts bring even more excitement to the new season.

Facing page: Decorated Wooden Eggs, page 67

DECOUPAGE FLOWER PLATE

Make this pretty plate with dried flowers from your own garden, or purchased flowers from the craft store. It's a unique way to serve your favorite bars or cookies, or it makes a beautiful floral display when set on an easel or plate stand.

Any size clear glass plate that you can find can be used for this project. Photographed is an 8-inch round dessert plate, but a dinner plate or serving platter would be beautiful too.

The flowers are very delicate, so working with a tweezers was helpful. You will be working on the bottom of the plate, not on the top, serving surface of the plate. Remember to turn the flowers upside down on the bottom of the plate so the pretty "front" of the dried flower is what you see when you look at the plate. Some flowers are bulky and don't work well for this project, especially for the very bottom of the plate where it has to sit on the table. Choose the flattest flowers possible when working on the bottom of the plate. Adding some greens and smaller flowers such as baby's breath helps give the plate an airier look.

This plate is not dishwasher safe, so remember to hand wash only the top of the plate with the least amount of water possible.

This project will take about five to seven hours (this includes drying time), for a cost of $30 to $35.

1 Remove all labels and wash plate thoroughly with soap and water. Trace around your plate and cut a circle of paper the same size as your plate on a piece of white scrap paper. Arrange flowers on circle of paper the way you will want them to be placed on the plate. Set plate on top of circle and dried flowers to get an idea of how your finished plate will look.

2 Turn plate over and paint one coat of decoupage medium on about $\frac{1}{3}$ of the bottom of the plate. Use tweezers to transfer dried flowers from your sample circle to bottom of plate. Remember to turn flowers over so the "front" of each flower is facing up. Continue $\frac{1}{3}$ at a time; let dry. Apply two additional coats of the decoupage solution to seal flowers onto plate; let dry between each coat for at least an hour.

3 Tear one sheet of Mulberry paper into small, irregular pieces, about 2 by 2 inches. Apply one coat of decoupage medium to the bottom of the plate. Adhere torn Mulberry paper to back of plate. This will seal up the bottom of the plate and has a nice, transparent look; let dry. Apply one more coat to seal all. Turn plate upside down and use a very sharp mat knife to cut excess Mulberry paper away from the rim of the plate.

PAPER-WRAPPED VOTIVE

With the arrival of spring comes the opportunity for entertaining outdoors on your deck, patio or porch again. There's nothing like the soft glow of candles in the evening to set a calm, relaxing atmosphere for you and your guests.

Materials & Tools

- Straight-sided glass votive or chimney candle-holder
- Mod Podge or other decoupage medium
- Rayon paper or opaque paper found in art supply stores
- Decorative cord or ribbon, beads and charms for embellishments
- Glue
- Decoupage medium applicator
- Scissors
- Measuring tape

These glass votive candleholders give off a beautiful glow while also protecting the candles from blowing out when they're on your porch or deck. They're very easy to make and can be used over and over again. Choose any size glass votive, round or square.

There are many different types of paper you can use. Mulberry paper, vellum paper and other handmade papers are affordable and easy to work with. The beautiful paper used in the photo is rayon paper. Art supply stores, scrapbooking stores and craft stores have hundreds of colors and patterns of papers to choose from. An opaque paper is best so the candle can glow from within. You can purchase a colored paper or paint your rayon paper with thinned acrylic paints to add more color and glow.

A colored candle will also add interest to the look. The embellishments you choose allow you to give the candleholder a theme such as butterflies, gardening or flowers. I used beads and garden charms on a cord to give the candle a finished look.

This project will take about two to three hours to make, for a cost of about $20 to $25.

1 Remove any labels and wash the glass well with soap and water. Let dry.

Measure the circumference of the glass chimney or votive with a strip of paper and add 1 inch for overlap. Cut the decorative paper the same length as the strip of paper and approximately 1 inch longer than the height of your glass.

Spread a thin layer of decoupage solution onto glass. Wrap paper around circumference of glass votive, aligning paper at the top edge of the glass. The bottom of the glass will now have an extra inch of paper.

2 Smooth the paper over the glass with your fingers, releasing any air bubbles. Apply a thin layer of glue to the overlap where the paper meets around the glass. Smooth the overlap down and let the glass dry upside down.

3 Cut slits in the paper at the bottom of the candle about 1 inch apart from each other and apply glue to the paper. Press the slits down and adhere onto the bottom of the glass votive one strip at a time. Smooth out any air bubbles with your fingers; let dry.

4 Measure around the top of the votive with your decorative cord and add a few extra inches onto the length so the ends can dangle down the front of the votive. Add beads and charms on the ends of the cord or ribbon to give a finished look. Use a drop of glue on the back of the cord at the back of the candle to attach to the top of the candle.

PLACE CARD HOLDER

This place card holder, made with a 2-inch clay pot, can also be used as a party favor. Everything is made of elements that remind us of spring — pussy willows, forsythia, twigs, bird's nest, butterfly and ladybug. This is a very quick and easy project ... and beautiful to behold.

The cost of the elements for this project is minimal, making it a great project to make in quantity for a party. It also is quick. One place card holder takes less than a half hour, so making multiples will go even faster per pot.

The cost of the nest, eggs and butterfly is approximately $1.12; however, most packages contain more than the amount needed for one project. The clay pot is about $0.50 and a large quantity of floral foam, Spanish moss and pussy willows (if purchased) is about $7.00 but will make many place card holders. The more you make the more the price per card holder goes down.

1 Cut floral foam with serrated knife to fit into the clay pot. Cut the piece of foam to 2 inches in depth, using a sawing motion.

Trace the top of the pot on scrap paper. Cut out pattern about ¼ inch smaller. This is a good place to start for the size of the floral foam.

Trace the pattern on top side of foam. Cut around the circle slicing downward and angling slightly inward. These cuts do not have to be in a circle; they will resemble an octagon and do not have to be even, as it will be covered. Try the foam in the pot. The foam should be a bit below the rim of the clay pot. You may need to continue cutting some of the foam away in small increments. Also the bottom of the foam may need to be cut away a bit to make the foam the right height.

Materials & Tools

- 2-inch clay pot
- Floral foam
- Small bird nest — 1½ inches
- Small eggs — ½ inch - three
- Butterfly or ladybug — ¾ inch
- Spanish moss
- Twigs — at least two — 6 to 7 inches high
- Pussy willow and/or blossom stem — 7 to 8 inches high
- Grapevine tendrils — small pieces, if desired
- Old pincher clothespin
- Round toothpick
- Glue gun and glue sticks
- Sharp serrated knife

2 Pull a small handful of Spanish moss from bag of moss. It should be an amount to cover the top of the pot. Put glue from glue gun over top of foam and the top edge of the pot. Place the moss on top of pot and gently press down. Trim any excess tendrils of moss.

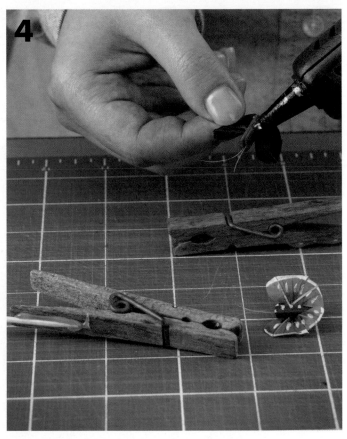

3 Add nest to the left of the top. Some nests are wired and the wire can be placed through moss and into foam. If the bird's nest is not wired, attach using glue gun.

Glue in three eggs or the amount to fill the nest. Add two to three twigs to the back and off-center behind nest. Add one piece of pussy willow about 7 to 8 inches high as the focal point. Add some grapevine tendrils to hang over the edge, if desired.

4 Using glue gun, put a line of glue on the outside of one of the handles on the clothespin and attach about half the length of the toothpick. Let dry.

Glue butterfly or ladybug on other side of clothespin, about halfway up. Push toothpick into clay pot to the right of the twigs and pussy willows. Be sure to place toothpick to allow enough room for the place card when placed into clothespin.

Craft Tip

- If using natural pussy willows and one of the blossoms falls off, glue it back on by placing a drop of glue on the area where if fell off and attach the blossom. Hold for a moment to dry.

COPPER DOORKNOB VASE

This conical-shaped "vase" gives any doorknob an intriguing new look. It is decorative and unique ... and fun to make. Much of the fun comes in choosing and decorating with beads. Copper will patina or discolor, adding to the charm.

The metal sheet can be purchased at a craft store. It is sized to take advantage of one 8- by 10-inch piece of metal. Metal edges are very sharp. Use caution when handling and cutting metal, and wear leather gloves or tape edges with masking tape. Also, wear safety glasses when cutting metal as a precautionary measure.

The finished dimensions of the "vase" are 6½ inches high, plus handle, and 4 inches in diameter. Use a variety of medium-sized beads in addition to the smaller-sized main beads.

The cost of the copper sheet and two sizes of copper wire are about $10 unless you have scraps of copper wire. The beads vary a lot in price, especially the medium-sized ones and large one, so the cost can be from $5 and up.

Be sure that the 18-gauge wire will fit through the holes in these beads. Take the wire with you when purchasing them. Choose the pony beads in a main color that will tie the color scheme together. This project will take a bit over one hour.

1 Make pattern from a thin piece of cardboard by making ¼ of a circle with radius of 8 inches. Cut pattern. Place pattern on corner of metal sheet and trace it with a felt-tipped marker. Mark location of holes to be made as follows: All marks are ¼ inch from edges. On each straight edge, make two holes at the top and two at the bottom, ⅜ inch apart. Be sure to be accurate as the holes will need to line up after bending the metal into a cone. Mark one hole at bottom circular edge equidistant from straight edges. At top rounded edge, measure 1½ inches in from marks on each straight edge, and mark. Then mark holes every inch until reaching the 1½-inch mark on other end.

Be sure project is on a board and punch holes at marks with an awl and hammer.

Materials & Tools

- Copper or tin sheet — 8 by 10 inches
- 24-gauge wire — (thin) about 36 inches
- 18-gauge wire — (thicker) about 36 inches
- Pony beads — size 5 — one small package
- Medium-sized beads — ¼ to ½ inch round or oval — about 12
- Medium-sized beads — ¼ to 1 inch oblong or tubular — about 5
- Large bead — about ⅝ inch, round or oval — 1
- Thin cardboard for pattern
- Felt-tipped marker
- Small bowl
- Tin snips
- Awl
- Needle-nose pliers
- Hammer
- Wire cutters

2 Gently work metal piece into cone shape. Line up the holes on straight edges. Cut two pieces of thicker wire about 3 inches long. Fold in half, going through the two holes from outside of cone to inside of cone.

Use needle-nose pliers to pull wire through and twist wire to hold secure. Press wire ends over edge and to outside of cone. This is the back and will not show. Do the same with the two holes at the bottom.

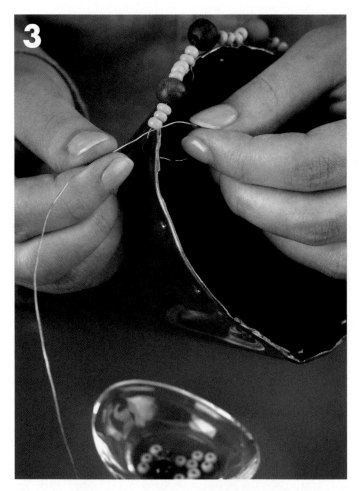

3 Select beads and place them in a small bowl. Using about 30 inches of thin wire and starting at the back of cone in hole that is 1½ inches from center back (hole 1), loop the end of the wire through hole and twist securely. Place three pony beads, one medium round or oval bead and three pony beads on wire. Thread wire into next hole from front (outside of cone) to inside; tighten so beads go along top of metal. Thread wire back over top and loop through wire and pull taut. Continue wrapping in this manner until the last hole is reached (hole 10). Loop wire through hole twice and secure.

4 To make handle, cut about 20 inches of thicker wire. Fold in half and thread through hole 10. Twist wires for about 1 inch and then add oblong or oval bead. Twist a few times. Add another bead to the wire that did not go through the last bead and twist. Add beads in this manner until about 2 inches from end. Twist for one more inch and loop through hole 1; secure by twisting.

Cut 3 inches of thicker wire and twist end around tip of the needle-nose pliers to make a curlicue. Put a pony bead on the wire, then large bead and another pony bead. Make a hook at the top and hook it through front hole at bottom of cone. Secure with needle-nose pliers.

Craft Tip

• Wear leather gloves and cut metal with tin snips. Any sharp edges can be hammered down later. Do not worry about unevenness, since most of the edges will not show in the final project.

DECORATED WOODEN EGGS

Decorating eggs is an Easter tradition, but why spend all your time on real eggs that won't last? Wooden eggs also have more texture from the wood grain, and can be painted beautifully. Use decorated wooden eggs in the ways traditional Easter eggs are used ... except for eating, of course! They can be used in a basket, or hung in a window or from a sign, such as the Happy Easter Sign on page 94.

These eggs are meant to be "Folk Art" in design and do not have to be executed with precision. The cost of 5 eggs using 5 paint colors would be about $10.00 and will take a few hours, due to drying time and practice time.

The following techniques of freehand design, sponging and color-washing are just a few you can try with this project. Take advantage of the wood grain, especially with the color-washed eggs. For the rest of the techniques, paint the eggs in a base coat of white or experiment on a wood board with other base-coat colors, such as robin's egg blue.

To make it easier to hold the eggs when painting, drill a hole in the wide end of egg and put in an eyelet screw. Also, it is easiest to hang the eggs to dry, using a hook, or one made from a paper clip, for each egg.

These 2-inch eggs are purchased at a craft store. They come in varying sizes, but this size is easy to handle.

Use craft acrylic paints in spring or Easter colors; experiment with various color combinations on a practice board painted in the base color. Especially for the freehand design, practice until you feel comfortable with the look.

1 Drill hole in wide end of eggs with very small bit. Put in eyelet screw. Do not apply a base coat to eggs to be color-washed. To apply base coat, hold screw and paint, letting each egg hang to dry between coats. Paint a practice board with base coat also.

2 **Freehand Designs:** These are very simple designs and can be mastered easily. Practice on the board, using different color combinations.

Start with vertical lines, using widest brush (about ⅛ inch). Let dry. Cross lines with another color, using a smaller brush for a check design. Try doing the cross lines while vertical lines are a bit wet for another "look."

Practice the zigzag pattern and dots. Dots are done by using the end of a chopstick or small dowel dabbed in the paint and applied. Dots can be thick or thin. When happy with the designs and color combinations, paint the eggs. Be sure to support both arms while painting and move the egg, not the brush. Remember the goal is not to be precise; a bit of variation is good. Hang to dry between adding colors or designs.

Speckled Egg: Do not use the eyelet screw; set egg on the flat side. Put some paint on paper plate. Practice speckling on board, by pulling an old toothbrush across the chopstick or dowel. Do only a few passes at a time and remove the built-up paint from the chopstick. A few bigger spots or even drizzles add to the design. Speckling in two colors also works well. Let dry and lay egg on side to get bottom areas of egg. Let dry.

Color-washed: Use eggs without base coat. Mix desired color with two parts paint and one part water. Apply color to egg with sponge brush. With paper towel, remove some of the wash so that the wood grain shows through.

3 **Sponged Eggs:** Put desired paint on paper plate. Using an area of the sponge with smaller holes, dab it in the paint and apply to practice board. Try different colors or one color on top of the other. Using a colored and darker base coat sponged with a lighter color is another variation. When happy with combinations, sponge eggs and hang to dry.

Craft Tip

• Spray all eggs with an acrylic sealer. When dry, remove eyelet screws or leave in for hanging eggs.

Seed-Saver Decorative Box

Have a special decorative place to keep seeds saved from your garden or ones received from friends. This tin box with lid has seed packet fronts decoupaged on the front and top. Inside is a divided tray to help keep your seeds separated, plus the lower part can be used for extra seed packets. Get all organized for spring planting!

Make your own decoupage medium by diluting white glue with a little water. Purchase a tin box with lid at a craft store and use your own seed packets to decorate the outside of the box. Making the divided tray with corrugated cardboard is easy.

The major cost of this project is the tin box, and it ranges from $6 to $10. The remaining items cost about $5 with plenty of wrapping paper left over. The project will take less than an hour with a little drying time.

Materials & Tools

- Tin box with lid — at least 6 inches long by 4 inches high by 4 inches wide
- Wrapping paper with a floral design
- White glue
- Thick corrugated cardboard (about ¼ inch) — a small piece
- Thin corrugated cardboard (about ⅛ inch) — an 8- by 10-inch piece
- Masking tape
- Clear tape
- Seed packets — at least three
- Brush — about ½ inch wide
- Small bowl
- Ribbon — the length of box plus about 5 inches
- Utility knife
- Glue gun and glue sticks
- Square or T-square

1 Make a mixture of white glue plus a little water in a small bowl.

Cut seed packets apart, using only the front. Arrange packets with two placed on the front of the tin box and one on the cover. Use more if the box is bigger. Place them at an angle for more interest. When happy with the placement, apply white glue medium to surface and place seed packet in position. Run a finger over the surface of the seed packet and especially along the edges, smoothing it. The glue will wrinkle the paper a bit, but that is part of the appeal.

Remove any of the liquid around edges with a damp paper towel. Let the box dry.

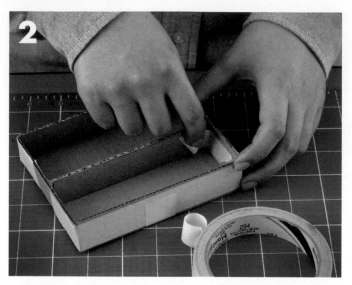

2 Measure the length of the inside front and back panels of the box. If the corners are rounded, measure only the flat surface. Measure the height of the inside front and back of the box and subtract 1½ inches from this measurement. Cut two pieces of the thick cardboard this size.

Place a cardboard piece on the front panel, 1½ inches below top edge, and glue with glue gun. Do this on the back panel also. Measure from the inside front to the inside back and subtract ⅛ inch. Measure from one inside side to the other and add 1½ inches.

Cut the thin cardboard to this measurement. Measure 1 inch in from each short edge and score (do not cut all the way through). Fold these 1-inch ends up. Cut two pieces of thin cardboard, 1⅛ inches high by the length of the cardboard with the ends turned up. Make a tray of these pieces and tape corners with masking tape. Check to make sure it fits inside the box. Measure from the inside of tray lengthwise. Cut one piece of thin cardboard that measurement by 1 inch high. Center in tray and tape in place with masking tape to make divider.

3 Cut strips of wrapping paper the inside length of the tray by at least several times the width of the tray. Fold paper in half, and place center over the divider. Check to see if it is a good fit.

Paint glue medium over divider and bottom of tray. Put wrapping paper over divider and smooth. Add the glue medium to rest of area to cover and smooth paper over it, going around to the outside bottom of tray.

Measure from inside tray to divider and cut three pieces of thin cardboard this measurement by 1 inch high. On one side place two dividers, equidistant from one another. Tape in place with clear tape. Cut two strips of wrapping paper the width of the remaining dividers to be covered. Cut an adequate amount to go over dividers and around to outside bottom of tray. Apply glue medium to tray starting from the middle out, smoothing wrapping paper into place. Cut a strip of wrapping paper 1½ inches wide by a length to wrap around the outside of the tray and overlap. Glue in place with glue medium. Cut a piece of coordinating ribbon the length of the tray plus about 5 inches. Glue lengthwise to outside bottom of tray, centering ribbon. This is to be used as a "handle" to lift tray out. Let everything dry.

Craft Tip
• Wallpaper or fabric may also be used to cover the tray.

Spring Tote

Decorate a carryall tote for shopping at the market, or to bring essentials along for a day at the park. You will be sure to find many uses for this versatile bag.

Here is unique way to use those beautiful photos taken in spring to embellish a practical craft project.

Purchase a packet of 8½- by 11-inch sheets of quick-fuse ink-jet fabric at an arts and crafts store. These can be printed with a color ink-jet printer or copier. They are very easy to use and provide great instant results. You will find many fun ways to decorate with these fabric photo transfers.

The tote can be completed in about 45 minutes; the materials needed will cost about $18.

Materials & Tools

- 14-inch by 13-inch canvas tote
- Washable quick-fuse 8½- by 11-inch ink-jet fabric sheets
- ½-inch width ribbon
- ½-inch double-stick permanent bond fusible web tape
- Fray Block
- Computer
- Ink-jet printer
- Digital photo file (or if you will be using a color copier, only a photo print will be needed)
- Iron
- Ironing board
- Scissors

1 Read and follow the instructions on the back of the package of the quick-fuse ink-jet fabric sheets. Select a digital image by scanning a printed photo, have a printed photo scanned onto a disk at a photo lab, or import an image that has been taken with a digital camera. Print the image onto the fabric side of the sheet.

If you do not have a computer and printer, you can easily use a color copier instead. Use one at your local copy store to make the copies. To use a color copier, load the quick-fuse fabric sheet into the paper tray. Place your printed photo on the copier. Copy the image onto the fabric side of the sheet. Allow the image to dry.

Craft Tip

- Apply a little Fray Block to the ends of the ribbon to keep the ribbon from unraveling. Allow it to dry.

2 Trim the image to the appropriate dimensions using scissors. The edges do not have to be cut perfectly straight; they will be covered by ribbon.

Place the tote on an ironing board and place your photo.

In this example, the photo is placed 3 inches from the top of the bag and 3 inches from the sides. Set the iron on a medium-high heat. Press for approximately 5 to 10 seconds. Make sure all areas are fused and secure.

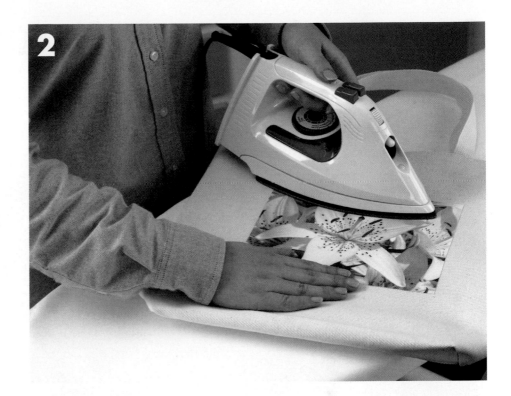

3 Measure the height and width of the photo to determine the lengths needed for the ribbon trim.

In this example, the photo measures 6 by 8 inches. Add an extra ½ inch to each of the four pieces of ribbon to miter the corners. This will create a more finished appearance.

Apply the double-stick fusible web tape to all four pieces of ribbon.

Peel off the release paper and attach the ribbon on top of the edges of the photo, overlapping at the corners.

Use scissors to cut the end of one piece of ribbon at an angle at the corner (approximately a 45-degree angle).

Cut the next piece of ribbon using the first cut ribbon as a

guide. Continue to do all four corners. Set the iron on medium-high and iron each piece of ribbon for 10 to 15 seconds. Make sure all areas are fused and secure. It is recommended to wash the finished tote by hand in cold water using liquid fabric softener and lay flat to dry.

SPRING MEMORIES SHADOW BOX

A shadow box is the perfect place to display your favorite spring mementos. Fill your
shadow box with souvenirs that hold a special place in your heart.

Decorating a shadow box is a fun and creative way to spend an afternoon. Fill your shadow box with anything you like that fits inside, such as photographs, postcards, miniature adornments and more. The sky is the limit; consider using natural elements as well, such as dried flowers, pussy willow, pebbles or driftwood.

Whatever you decide to use, your shadow box will be one of a kind if you use elements that are meaningful to you and your loved ones. In one or two hours, this shadow box can be completed for $20 to $30.

1 Use decorative paper to decorate the rear wall of your shadow box. Try layering images of varying shapes and sizes over one another to create a stimulating tapestry of your favorite photographic memories. Polaroid pictures or images taken in photo booths create a whimsical and timeless appeal. If you don't have any, call some friends and go make some together; you'll be glad you did.

The most effective way to fasten images into the shadow box is using photo corners. Photo corners hold your picture in place with adhesive backing and affix them into position. Your local craft store may have many types of photo corners, including plain corners and specialty design corners.

2 When your pictures have been fastened on, layer additional decorative elements sporadically around your images using stickers, double-stick tape or a hot-glue gun.

Consider using dried flowers picked from your own garden, or purchase dried flowers at a specialty arts and paper store. Use flowers that flourish during the spring months. Some examples include daisies, violets and hyacinths.

Also consider affixing additional elements to your tapestry, such as handmade adornments as required to fill the space.

Craft Tip

- Design your shadow box display from the inside out toward the opening. In this way you can layer your box more efficiently without disturbing elements that you have already set carefully in place. This project will require a certain amount of testing and experimentation.

3 The bottom of the shadow box is a great place to rest three-dimensional objects. Fill the lower section of your box with pebbles and seashells to create an oceanic effect. Include sentimental ornaments intermingled with the pebbles to add personalization. Try including driftwood collected from the beach to accentuate the natural qualities of your showcase. Add pussy willow branches protruding throughout to create a splash of life.

SPRING VIOLETS FOR YOUR LAPEL

You can tell spring is in the air when fresh flowers start blooming, and some of the most colorful and vibrant flowers are pansies and violets. Now you can keep that spring feeling with you all year round by creating this colorful lapel pin.

Pressed flowers can be purchased at many paper goods stores, and now with the microwave flower press, flowers can easily be pressed at home too. It's a great feeling to wear your own garden flowers on your lapel. Pansies and violets come in every color imaginable, and each one is a work of art. There is no need to develop your painting skills to re-create these lovely flowers on a lapel pin. By using the dried, pressed flower to create a lapel pin, you can keep all the vibrant colors and exquisite detail of the flower to wear with your favorite spring outfit.

Because the product must dry thoroughly between steps, the whole process takes about three days. Flowers can be purchased for a few dollars or pressed at home. Paperclay, Mod Podge, acrylic spray, and adhesive pins or earring posts and fasteners can be purchased at a craft store for about $16 to $17. These supplies are enough to make a large number of lapel pins.

1 Place a piece of Paperclay between two pieces of plastic wrap and roll the clay to a thickness of about ⅛ inch. Remove the plastic wrap and place a pressed flower on top of the rolled clay. Using a razor knife, cut the clay around the outside edges of the flower.

Setting the flower aside, remove the excess clay and pat the edges of the cut mold until slightly rounded. Shape the flattened piece by pressing slightly in the center and pulling the edges up slightly to give the clay the suggestion of a flower shape. Allow the clay to dry overnight. If more than one flower is done at a time, keep the flower next to the mold it was cut for. Since each flower shape is slightly different, it will make matching each flower to the correct mold easier.

Materials & Tools

- Rolling pin
- Razor cutting knife
- Paintbrush
- Dried, pressed flowers
- Paperclay
- Mod Podge
- Emery board or fine sanding paper
- Crystal-clear acrylic coating spray
- E6000 adhesive
- Broach pin back
- Pierced earring posts and fastener backs (optional)

Craft Tips

- The finished lapel pin is great fun to wear and wonderful to give as a gift. A decorated gift card can be created to hold or display the pin by folding a 4- by 5-inch piece of card stock in half. Punch holes for the pin back using a paper punch. Stamp the card using stamping ink and an appropriate stamp for a spring gift. The card and lapel pin can also be used as a place setting decoration for a spring luncheon.

- The same process can be used to create "Spring Fling" earrings by selecting smaller flowers like the Johnny-jump-up violet. Instead of using a broach pin back, adhere a pierced earring post to the back of the finished clay/flower. The earrings also make a nice gift or table place setting decoration. Place a pair of earrings on a decorated, folded card with two holes punched using a tiny paper punch.

2 Maintain the flower flattened between two pieces of wax paper while clay is drying.

After the clay is dry, place the flower over the dried clay. If the edges of the clay show beyond the edges of the flower, sand the clay slightly with an emery board.

Using a small paintbrush, paint Mod Podge over the top of the clay. Press the flower in position over the painted clay, matching the edges of the flower and the edges of the clay.

Position the entire petal carefully in place. Spray the dried flower with the acrylic spray before you decoupage to prevent the color from fading during the decoupage process. Air dry. Paint Mod Podge over the top of the flower. Allow to dry overnight.

3 After the clay and Mod Podged flower are dry, sand any remaining edges of the clay up to the edge of the flower, using an emery board or very fine sandpaper. Also round the edges of the clay on the back side of the broach to create a smooth back.

Paint Mod Podge on the front, back and edges of the broach. Allow to dry overnight. Additional layers of Mod Podge may be added if necessary. Spray the broach with acrylic spray to finish and give a glossy coating.

After the spray is dry, apply E6000 adhesive to the back of the broach and press the broach pin back into the adhesive. If you

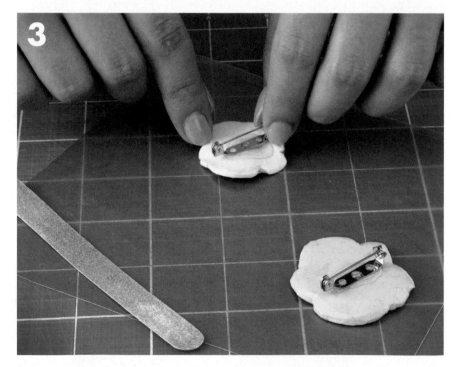

have smaller flowers that are not large enough by themselves, glue them with E6000 glue to the edge of a larger clay/flower to make a slightly larger lapel pin. Use a variety of colors and sizes of flowers to glue together. Allow to dry well before wearing.

Spring Mini-Quilt and Grandma's Garden Gate

It's fun to have a special place to decorate for each season by changing the articles on display. Here's a springtime start! The garden gate has special significance, as it is a replica of Grandma's garden gate.

Select a central idea or theme to display on your wire frame. Find a stamp that represents that theme. For spring, use fresh, bright flowers in a vase or growing up in a new garden. After stamping your special theme stamp on fabric, stitch it with embroidery floss in bright spring colors. Add colorful fabric borders and ribbon. Tie the mini-quilt on the wire rack as the central interest. Add candles, flowers or other special remembrances of spring and Grandma's home and garden.

The stitching of the stamped fabric square takes about one hour or more depending upon the complexity and size of the stamp selected. Embroidery floss and scraps of fabric or "fat quarters" are used for the picture and complementary fabric and can be purchased for a few dollars or made from old scraps of previous projects. If you are using favorite old stamps from previous projects, there is no additional cost involved. Otherwise, purchased stamps cost from $2 to $12, depending upon the size.

1 From light muslin or tea-stained fabric, and using a rotary cutter, mat and cutting ruler, cut a square or rectangle big enough to accommodate the stamp(s) and also allow you to put it in an embroidery hoop. Size may vary depending upon stamp or grouping. Stamp the selected picture on the fabric using washable ink. If you stamp the picture on crooked, just rinse off the ink by running warm water over it, press slightly dry in a towel, press and try again.

Place fabric in embroidery hoop and, using needle and embroidery floss, hand stitch the outline of the stamp using a backstitch. If the stamp has a colored picture on the back, use the stamp back to help select the color of the floss. When needed, use a French knot or satin stitch.

When all stitching is complete, rinse the fabric square to remove any ink that may be showing. Press the square. Trim the square with a rotary cutter to desired size, making sure to allow for ¼-inch seam.

Materials & Tools

- Scissors
- Needles
- Sewing machine
- Cutting mat
- Rotary cutter
- Cutting ruler
- Iron
- Spring stamps
- Embroidery hoop
- Scraps of light muslin or tea-stained fabric
- About ¼ yard of complementary fabric
- Light thread for sewing machine
- Embroidery floss
- Washable ink pad
- Scraps of quilt batting
- Ribbon
- Garden gate wire rack for display

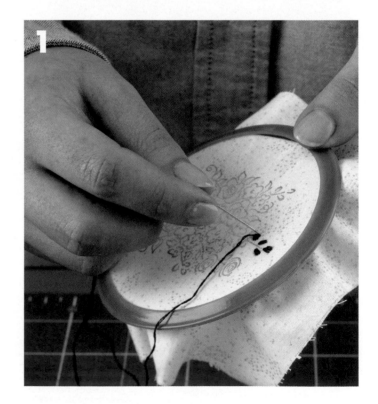

2 From a complementary fabric, cut one or two 1¾-inch strips to use for a border. The number of border pieces will depend on the size of the muslin square. Pin and sew the border to the top and bottom of the stamped square using a ¼-inch seam allowance. Trim ends of border even with the sides. Press seams to the outside. Then sew border to the left and right of the stamped square using a ¼-inch seam allowance. Trim ends of border to form a square or rectangle. Press seams to the outside.

Optional: A second border in another complementary fabric may also be added. Cut a 2½-inch border and sew to the first border starting at the top and bottom and then moving to the left and right of the first border.

3 Cut a square ¼ inch larger than top of finished mini-quilt from same fabric as first border. Cut a square of quilt batting about the same size. Layer and pin the hand-stitched square over the fabric square (with right sides together) and the quilt batting, matching the corners and sides. Stitch front to back on all sides using a ¼-inch seam allowance and leaving a small opening to turn the mini-quilt. Trim corners and turn inside out. Press.

Slipstitch the opening closed using a hemming stitch. Add an optional line of hand quilting just inside the border on the fabric with the hand-stitched picture. Tack ribbon to back of fabric. Tie quilt to wire rack with ribbons.

Craft Tips

- Simple outline stamps are best to allow plenty of definition in the stitching. Select pictures that have spring flowers like daffodils, larkspur, hydrangea, pansies, etc.

- Find complementary articles to display with the mini-quilt. Dipped candles are great for hanging over a wire rack. If you have Grandma's jewelry, you can display a special memory piece.

- If you have a garden, pick flowers and arrange in a bouquet. Dry the flowers by hanging upside down. For spring, select blue larkspur or yellow daffodils. While your garden is fresh, select flowers to dry for the other seasons to come. Red globe amaranth and white statice are great for winter. Purple, pink and white globe amaranth and purple, white and blue statice are great for summer. Colorful leaves are great for fall. Leaves can be dried using a microwave flower press before arranging in bouquet. Tie a larger, coordinating ribbon on the bouquet, and tie the bouquet to the wire rack.

SPRING DECORATING

Spring is a natural time to try some new decorating ideas. Bright light floods your home. Open windows let warm breezes in. Soft rainshowers wash everything clean. You want your home to look as fresh, vibrant and colorful as the world outside! So give these exciting decorating projects a little bit of your time and energy. You'll be pleased with yourself (for completing the projects) and with your home (for the wonderful new looks you've added).

Facing page: Decoupage Glass Containers, page 106

PAINTED FLOWER BUCKETS

Painted buckets make a nice change from terra-cotta pots, and provide a unique way to display flowers on your deck, porch or the steps leading up to your house. Paint the buckets to match the colors in your flower garden.

These functional buckets add a splash of color and cheer to your deck, patio or porch when filled with potted plants, herbs or cut flowers from your garden.

The buckets are very common and come in many different sizes and can be found in hardware stores, garden stores, import stores or flower markets. Purchase new buckets or search flea markets and antique stores for vintage buckets and paint them. Just be sure to steel wool the old buckets really well to remove any rust that may be on them.

Plant right in the bucket or use pots that are already planted set inside them. A vase or jar filled with cut flowers looks nice inside the bucket. Paint the buckets a solid color, then embellish them with rubber stamps or stencils in contrasting colors. Or paint them pastel or vibrant primary colors, depending on the look of your garden.

These buckets also work wonderfully to hold an herb garden on the deck or patio for those who enjoy container gardens. Alphabet stencils work well for stenciling the names of the herbs onto the buckets.

The project will take about two to three hours to make, for a cost of about $15 to $25.

Craft Tip

- If printing a word on the bucket with an alphabet stencil, draw a straight line where you want the word to go, then stencil the letters on the line to keep them straight.

1 Rub the bucket with steel wool to remove any dirt and oil and wash thoroughly with soap and water; let dry.

2 Paint entire outside of bucket and part of the way down inside of bucket; let dry. Add a second coat of paint; let dry again.

Add any embellishments you may like with a rubber stamp or stencil of your choice.

Paint a small amount of paint onto a rubber stamp with a brush and stamp the paint onto the bucket as you would with ink on paper. After the stamped design is dried, you can fill in any missed or thin paint spots with a small artists brush.

Materials & Tools

- Buckets purchased at garden store, craft store or antique store
- Steel wool
- Contrasting paint color (for stamp or stencil; optional)
- Stencil or rubber stamp (optional)
- Weather-resistant varnish
- Paint applicator
- Hammer
- Nail

3 Once the paint on the bucket is dry, turn the bucket upside down and punch 3 holes in the bottom of the bucket with a hammer and nail so that water can get out. Coat the outside and the inside of the bucket with a weather-resistant varnish to protect it from the elements and to keep it from chipping.

Mini-Screen Door Hanging

Hang this mini-screen door by the front door, on the door itself or on the porch, to greet springtime guests. Change the message hanging from the doorknob for different seasons and holidays.

To look authentic, this mini-screen door is made from weathered wood, an old-looking screen and a miniature knob for the sign to be hung. Greenery, such as ivy, could be added, as well as spring flowers, if desired.

When working with weathered wood, use irregularities as an advantage, thus enhancing the charm of this project. Also, weathered boards may not all be the same in width and depth, so cut the wood strips to advantage, from ¾ to 1 inch wide. The finished dimensions of the mini-screen door can vary from 16 by 6½ inches to 16 by 7½ inches, depending on the width of the wood strips. You may wish to cut the strips for the diagonals a bit narrower.

The screen can be purchased by the square foot at hardware stores, or use old screen. Often hardware stores have scraps of screen or even the old screen removed when fixing screens, at minimal or no charge at all. Old screen makes this project look more authentic, but using black screen, either painted aluminum or nylon, also works well.

Look for a miniature knob at hardware or home stores or a wood knob at craft stores. If using a wood knob, whitewash it to make it look older.

This project is inexpensive. Using available weathered board, purchased screen, a scrap for the sign and a purchased small knob, it will cost no more than $3, plus paint and picture hanger for back. The mini-screen door will take about an hour plus drying time.

Materials & Tools

- Weathered wood board measuring at least 3 by ¾ inch by at least 21½ inches
- Screen — old or black aluminum or black nylon, at least 16 by 7½ inches
- One small or miniature knob
- Craft wood — about ¼ inch thick by about 4½ by 2¾ inches
- White water-based paint — latex or acrylic craft paint
- Craft acrylic paint — in desired spring color for lettering
- Alphabet stencil — with letters about ¾ inch wide by 1 inch high
- Wood glue
- Small nails with large head — a few
- Carpet tacks or thumbtacks, or staple gun and staples
- String — about 6 inches
- Sponge brush
- Stencil brush
- Picture hanger
- Miter saw or handsaw and miter box
- Table saw
- Electric drill and small drill bit
- Rasp
- Clamps
- Hammer

1 With a table saw, cut weathered wood into three strips, ¾ inches wide, or to take advantage of the width of the wood, up to 1 inch wide. Measure and cut both outside strips to take advantage of using the weathered edges. Cut each outside strip into one 16-inch length and one 5½-inch length. Cut the center strip into one 5½-inch length. You may wish to make the remaining part of the strip a bit narrower. Then cut four 2¾-inch pieces with 45-degree angles, angling in, on each end.

2 Lay project on flat working surface, assembling as shown in photo. Glue at each joint and diagonal pieces. Clamp and let glue dry according to manufacturer's directions.

To further reinforce joints (diagonal ones do not need to be reinforced), drill a small hole at corners for nails, from the outside strip going into the cross (horizontal) strips. Pound nails into drilled holes. Measure width and height of project and cut screen a little less than that measurement. Place screen over wrong (back) side of project and tack or staple. Nail a picture hanger centered at top back of project. Add doorknob.

3 To prepare sign, cut craft board about 4½ inches by 2¾ inches. To make the sign look old, distress edges with a rasp or other tool to make it look worn.

Drill small holes at top corner of board about ⅜ inch from each edge. Whitewash surface with a mixture of two parts white water-based paint and one part water. Use one to two coats, as desired. Let each coat dry.

Mark placement of letters with a small strip of masking tape. Using a stenciling brush and stencil, apply acrylic paint, spelling out desired message, such as "Think Spring." Let each letter dry between stenciling. (This does not take long.) When dry, tie approximately a 6-inch length of string through holes and hang.

Craft Tip

• It is easiest to cut the angles while making the original 2¾-inch cut and using the cut angle as the next piece to cut. See photo 1.

TULIP STAMPED CAFÉ CURTAIN

You can create this project using a purchased sheer café curtain or a homemade one. The border is added and stamped, or you can stencil it with a tulip or other spring flower design. Use silk flowers to embellish the top of the curtain. To choose colors for this project, borrow a theme from one of the silk flowers.

If purchasing the sheer café curtains, simply purchase ones to fit your window. Making the café curtains requires basic sewing skills. This project can also be made with fusible web instead of sewing. Either way, purchase a small piece of fine white muslin for the border, on which the designs are stamped.

The stamp for this project is a chunky-type stamp. Purchase either textile paints or add textile medium to craft acrylic paints. Also use a gel blending medium to extend the drying time while stamping.

If sewing the curtains, measure the width of the window from the outside of the moldings and the height of the window to sill. Sheer fabric needed for the width will be 1½ to 2½ times the width plus 4 inches for hems by ½ the height of the window. Unless the window is very small, the amount of fabric needed would be twice the length or height of curtain. If the fabric is 44 inches wide, this project would take about 1½ yards of sheer fabric and 1 yard of cotton muslin. These amounts will be adequate for an average window. Pre-wash all fabric.

This project will cost $10 to $12 for fabric or purchased curtain plus about $8 for stamp and paint. It will take a couple of hours, depending on sewing skill.

Materials & Tools

- Sheer fabric (preferably cotton) — 44 inches wide — 1½ yards
- Fine white cotton muslin — 44 inches wide — 1 yard
- Chunky-type stamp — tulip design or other spring flower — about 2½ to 3½ inches high
- Textile or craft acrylic paints — green, yellow, dark yellow and an accent color
- Textile medium — if using craft acrylic paints
- Gel blending medium
- Paintbrushes — about ¼ inch wide — one for each color paint
- White thread
- Rings for top of curtain — 14 to 20
- Measuring tape
- Shears
- Fabric marker
- Hand sewing needle
- Café curtain rod — adjustable to fit window
- Sewing machine
- Iron

1 If making curtains, cut sheer fabric 1½ to 2½ times width of window plus 4 inches for hems. Cut the height about ½ height measurement of window. Cut the width in half, vertically, creating 2 panels, if desired. Make a double hem on each side of panels and at top. Fold ½ inch on each side on each panel, and then fold ½ inch again and press. Stitch close to the inside folded edge. Do the same at the top of each panel.

If using a purchased curtain, cut the hem off. If purchasing or making curtains, cut white muslin for border the width of the sheer curtain plus 2 inches for hem. Cut the height to be at least 2 inches plus height of stamp times two.

2 Measure a centered horizontal line on each muslin piece. Mark placement of each design with a fabric marker. Depending on size of design, space designs evenly. Prepare paints. Add textile medium to paint, if using acrylic paints. Practice stamping. Dip brush into blending medium and then into paint, working paint and medium into brush. Use one paintbrush per color. Paint desired colors on stamp. Place on practice fabric and press. When ready, stamp fabric, applying paint to stamp between each application of stamp. Add any desired freehand design elements between stamped designs. Let dry and press.

3 At bottom of curtain panel, place stamped panel, right sides together, with about 1 inch extending from each end of stamped panel. Sew a ½-inch seam. Press seam toward stamped panel. Fold sides into a double-fold hem, folded ends even with the sheer curtain panel. From wrong side, fold the remaining edge ½ inch down and press. Turn to the back of curtain, even with top of stamped panel. Pin. Topstitch close to top edge of stamped panel, making sure to catch fabric fold on back side. Equally divide top of curtain into 2- to 3-inch sections, mark and hand-sew rings to top of curtain. Press.

Hang and embellish with tulip buds or appropriate flower, if desired.

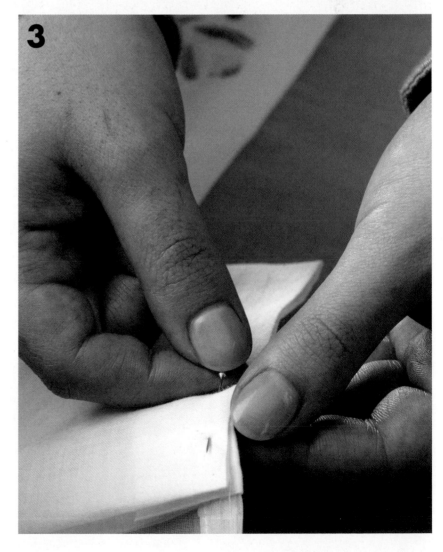

HAPPY EASTER SIGN

This sign will look great on a wall in your home, in the foyer, or on your front door or porch. It is easy to make, and uses five traditional Easter colors. The Decorated Wooden Eggs, another project from this book (page 67), are ideal to hang from the sign. Or hang any variety of Easter-themed wooden or metal cutouts, such as carrots, bunnies, chicks or plastic eggs.

The sign is made on a purchased 8- by 10-inch plaque, but can also be made from scraps of wood. Alphabet stamps or stencils can be used for the lettering. The alphabet style used is a bit whimsical, and the finished letters have a thick-and-thin look to enhance that effect.

A more traditional look can be achieved by using a traditional alphabet and stenciling, where the paint application can be more controlled.

The wooden cutouts on the sign can be in any Easter-related shape, and they can also be painted in the traditional colors. These were sponged; however, any of the techniques shown on the Decorated Wooden Eggs (page 67) will also work. When finished, the sign could be speckled.

The cost will depend on which type of plaque or homemade sign is used. This plaque was about $3. The remaining costs of wood cutouts and paint are about $6, and the ribbon can also vary from bargain bin to a few dollars. It will take several hours plus drying time between coats of paint.

Materials & Tools

- Wooden plaque — about 8 by 10 inches or one from wood scraps
- Alphabet sponge letters in about 1¼-inch or alphabet stencils
- Wood buttons — ½ inch (purchased at a craft store, these are not sewing buttons)
- Wooden cutouts — half eggs (as shown), about three, or other cutouts
- Latex paint — blue and white
- Craft acrylic paint — any of the desired Easter colors, such as lavender, green, blue, turquoise, yellow, pink
- Ribbon — ¾ inch, about 3 yards and ¼ inch, about 1½ yards — in an Easter color
- Brads — ¾ inch — five
- Stencil brush
- Tools for desired painting technique, such as sponging, as shown
- Sponge brush for painting plaque
- Masking tape
- Wood glue
- Spray acrylic sealer in matte or gloss
- Hammer
- Drill and about ¼-inch drill bit

1 Drill holes in the upper corners of plaque, about ¼ inch from each flat edge. Sand plaque, if needed, and smooth around holes. Paint edges with two coats of white paint. Let dry between coats.

Tape edges. Apply two coats of blue paint and let dry between coats. Remove masking tape.

2 Decide the placement of the letters and use masking tape to mark a lower edge guideline. The first line of letters is 3½ inches from the top of plaque and the first "P" is centered. The second line of letters is 2 inches below the first line and the "E" starts about ¾ inch in from left edge.

Place paint on a paper plate and make into a circle of paint large enough for the stamp. Practice the letter placement on a paper, to confirm the above measurements or adjust them.

Place stamp in paint and dab on plate. Check to make sure the paint has covered the stamp and is not too thick. A thick-and-thin application is okay for the look of whimsy. When comfortable, apply stamp firmly to project. Remove tape when done with each line.

3 Paint the wood cutouts and wood buttons with a base coat of white. Let dry. Apply desired technique to decorate them. Let dry.

Decide on placement of wood cutouts. The five wood buttons are placed about ½ inch from bottom edge and start and end at ½ inch from side edges, with about 2 inches between buttons. Glue wood cutouts on sign. Place a brad at center of wood button and hammer into button only until the point reaches the bottom of button. Add wood glue sparingly to bottom of wood button and place on sign. Nail in place. Finish applying wood buttons.

Apply a dab of paint the color of the sponging, to cover the head of each brad. Spray with an acrylic sealer. Cut wide ribbon about 44 inches to hang sign. Thread or push through holes and double the ribbon, tying a bow at the top. Cut five 12-inch pieces of wide ribbon for bow above egg, and about five 10-inch pieces of narrow ribbon for loops to hang eggs. Thread narrow ribbon through eyelet and tie with knot. Hang on sign to check desired length. Eggs may be hung to be level or to vary in length, as desired. Tie a small bow at the top of the egg. Repeat for all eggs.

Craft Tip

• Little drying time is needed between each letter application.

Ivy Basket Topiary

Try this new twist on a classic idea. Ivy abounds in spring, so make your own unique topiary
to give as a gift or to decorate almost any room in your home.

Welcome spring with a beautiful ivy basket display. Create numerous different shapes and forms using armature wire as the frame.

This kind of wire can be found in bulk at an art store. It is very easy to bend into shape. Try using other varieties of vines, such as the grape ivy, for a different effect.

You will spend from two to three hours and about $60 on this topiary basket.

1 Read and follow instructions for the two-step natural rust painting kit to use on the wire basket.

Spray the basket with the textured base coat. Allow it to dry. Dilute a small amount of the top coat with an equal amount of water in a disposable cup. Mix the two together. Brush on the top coat with the sponge brush from the kit. Immediately remove some of the top coat with a lint-free rag, blotting randomly. Allow it to dry.

Craft Tip

- Make sure the ivy plant has good drainage by either purchasing a saucer with reservoirs to collect water drainage or place a layer of rocks in the saucer to keep the pot from sitting in water.

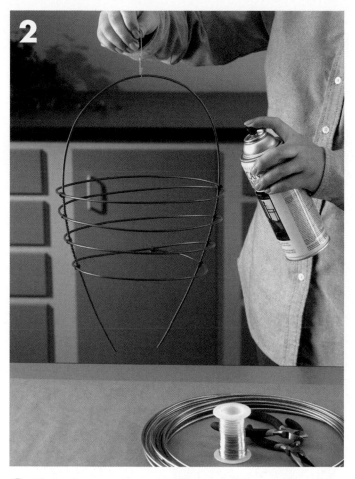

2 Use wire cutters to cut 10 feet of armature wire for the body of the basket. Shape the body of the basket in an upward spiral, making the top larger than the bottom. Make a small bend at the bottom end of the wire using needle-nose pliers. This will help keep the bottom two ribs (the horizontal tiers of wire) wired in place together. Use about 5 inches of 24-gauge wire to wrap tightly around the bottom piece of wire and the next tier of wire. Repeat this step to the top of the basket.

Cut another piece of armature wire 3 feet long for the handle. Bend into a handle-shaped curve. Leaving about 5 inches of wire at the bottom of each end (to use as spikes to insert into the potted dirt). Wrap a 3-foot piece of 24-gauge wire in a crisscross method around each rib and handle frame. Then twist the wire around the handle frame once or twice and repeat to crisscross around each rib. Finish by crisscrossing twice at the top of the basket around the handle frame. Cut off excess wire. Repeat this step to the other side of the handle frame. Bend a paper clip into an S-shape to hang the basket onto for spray painting. Spray paint the completed basket form with green spray paint. Allow it to dry.

3 Take sheets of moss and line the inside of the rust-painted wire basket. Place a saucer at the bottom. Place the potted ivy plant on top of the saucer. Gather up the ivy vines and insert the spikes from the formed wire basket into the dirt (having the plant now inside the basket). Wrap each of the ivy vines around the wire ribs spiraling up the basket and around the handle. Place more moss on top to completely conceal the pot.

TEAPOT FLORAL ARRANGEMENT

Refine an old teapot, or resurrect one that has a broken lid, and make it into a cheery spring floral arrangement with a candle in the center. Use spring blossoms such as apple, cherry or plum for the taller elements. Incorporate tulip, iris, lilac or daffodil blossoms for the shorter elements around the arrangement's outside edge.

The teapot needs to be a 2-cup or larger one and can be plain or with a floral design.

If you do not have a teapot to use for this project, look for one at a thrift shop or garage sale. Use an old, short wooden candleholder or make one from a wooden candle cup from a craft store and attach it to a flat base that will fit inside the pot.

Determine your color scheme before shopping for floral stems and candle. If the teapot has a design on it, pick colors from that design.

The cost of this project is around $6, not including the teapot. The cost of the silk flowers may range a lot. It will take less than an hour to complete this project.

1 Determine size of candle needed and floral stems or bushes needed. If using a smaller, shorter teapot, use a slimmer, smaller candle. You may need to place a small block of floral foam in the bottom of the teapot, secured under the candleholder to add height. Cut pieces of floral foam a bit smaller than the inside of the pot and about an inch in depth, unless using a taller teapot. Cut the square in half and take out a bit of the center to allow for the candleholder. This will allow the piece of foam to fit around candleholder and go through the opening of the teapot.

2 Using a glue gun, glue candleholder to center of bottom inside of teapot. Glue pieces of floral foam around candleholder. Determine the height needed for the taller blossoms and cut to that length. Place into floral foam near and surrounding the candle. Glue with glue gun, if necessary.

3 Determine the height needed for the blossoms for the outer ring of flowers and cut to that length. Save any leaves from the stems for inserting into arrangement as needed. Place stems into floral foam creating a circle of flowers around the first row and near the rim of the teapot. Glue with glue gun, if necessary. Place leaves in arrangement as needed. If using a larger teapot, another row of stems may be needed to make it a full arrangement. Style the blossoms and leaves. As the finishing touch, place a ribbon around the lip of the teapot if it has one and if there is no design on the teapot.

Materials & Tools

- Teapot
- Flower stems — tall slender blossoms — about six stems, depending on the size of the teapot
- Flower stems — bush or blossoms such as iris, lilac, etc. — about six blossoms or one bush
- Floral foam — one brick
- Ribbon — several feet
- Wooden candleholder
- Candle — 12 inch, unless using a larger teapot — dripless
- Wire cutter
- Glue gun and glue sticks
- Serrated knife

Craft Tip

- To remove any glue tendrils, use a blow dryer and they will disappear.

FRAMED WIRE WALL VASE

Create an attractive hanging vase to display springtime floral arrangements on your wall.

This simple and elegant accent can help decorate any room in your home.

This quick-and-easy home decorating craft will be sure to add a pleasing touch to any room. Bring a little spring inside your home. Fill the vase with an arrangement of pussy willows, cherry blossoms, stargazer lilies, calla lilies, tulips, irises or larkspur as some wonderful possibilities. Or use these vases to display a lovely dried flower arrangement. Whether they are made as a gift or for your own home, they will be sure to brighten anyone's day. This project will take about 30 minutes to make, for a cost of about $60 (including the staple gun).

1 Disassemble the backing and glass from the frame. These pieces will not be needed to create this craft. Wire mesh will be stapled directly to the back of the frame. Measure the wire mesh ¾ inch larger on all sides of the frame's window. Take a ruler to measure and mark the wire mesh with the cut lines. Use scissors to cut out the appropriate size wire mesh for the window. Carefully handle the wire as it will be rough on the edges.

2 On the back of the frame, lay the wire mesh centered on the frame's window. Use a staple gun to secure the wire mesh to the back of the frame. Safety glasses are recommended. Load the gun with ¼-inch staples. Shoot the staples near the edge of the wire mesh beginning at the corner, leaving them about 1 inch apart. Be sure to secure each corner with one staple as you go around.

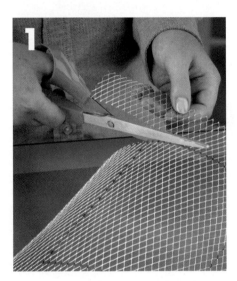

3 Cut a piece of 14-inch, 24-gauge wire using a ruler to measure and wire cutters to cut the wire. Wrap the wire around the vase ⅔ up from the bottom. Twist the wire together and continue twisting the remaining wire. Pull the twisted wire through an opening at the middle of the bottom row going across the wire mesh. Wearing safety glasses, shoot a staple onto the wire to the back of the frame. If there is plenty of extra wire, you can cut it off using wire cutters. Leave a small amount extra to wind up into a ball to staple above, firmly anchoring the wired vase in place. Tie a ribbon around the vase concealing the wire underneath. Cut off excess ribbon. Finally, place a floral arrangement in the vase.

Materials & Tools

- 4- by 6-inch weathered or crackled picture frame
- Fluted shooter vase or mini bud vase
- ½-inch pattern aluminum wire mesh (found at an arts and crafts store)
- 24-gauge wire — 14 inches
- Ribbon — 1 yard
- Staple gun
- ¼-inch staples
- Wire cutter
- Safety glasses
- Scissors
- Ruler
- Marker

SPRING MAGNETS

Adorn your fridge with personalized magnets! Create fun shapes from vegetables, fruits and flowers that celebrate the spring season.

These precious magnets help display all those photos and mementos on the fridge. Add personality to your magnets by creating them by hand. Create a series of fun shapes for each of the four seasons. Mix the exact color you are looking for to create a wider range of colors.

This project's charm is all in the details. Three or four different shapes can be created in about 1½ hours at a cost of about $15, which includes a clay stylus tool.

1 These instructions will explain how to create the peas in a peapod magnet. Every shape will be unique as part of the process.

Prepare your work surface by taping a sheet of wax paper to your table.

Using a craft knife, cut ⅛ of a package of pearl-colored clay and 1/16 of a package of leaf green-colored clay. Knead the two colors on your work surface using the palm of your hand. Blend until uniformly colored.

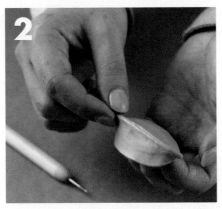

2 Roll out two pieces of the same size clay, leaving enough clay to create about six peas after making the pod. Push down to flatten and form into the shape of the two sides of a pod. Use the handle of the stylus as a "rolling pin" to help flatten the clay. Join the two sides and pinch the bottoms together. Open the pod and flip it over. Using your finger, smooth down the pinched seam.

Materials & Tools

- Polymer oven-bake clay (peas in a peapod: leaf green and pearl)
- ½-inch-diameter magnet buttons
- Double-ended stylus
- Craft knife
- Hot-glue gun
- Glue sticks
- Wax paper
- Tape
- Baking pan
- Tinfoil

3 Mix a little more of the pearl-colored clay to the remaining green clay to give a slight variation in color from the pod to the peas. Roll out about six peas, making the peas at the ends smaller than the peas in the middle. Place the peas inside the pod. Use the stylus to help set the peas in place. Using your finger, push between each pea to add more shape to the peapod. Flip over and repeat.

Place your shapes on a baking pan lined with tin foil. Bake at 275°F for 15 to 30 minutes per ¼-inch thickness. After the shapes have cooled, use a hot-glue gun to adhere a magnet to the back of each shape.

DECOUPAGE GLASS CONTAINERS

Make a stylish set of glass containers to hold your cotton swabs, cotton balls or other bathroom accessories. This attractive set complements almost any bathroom décor.

Decoupage pressed ferns, leaves or flowers to the containers. These could also be used as candle holders instead.

Purchase pressed plants and flowers at a craft store or make them at home.

Put a piece of blotting paper on top of an open page in a phone book. Place your floral specimens on the blotting paper, making sure they are not overlapping. Put another piece of blotting paper on top. You can insert several of these between the pages of one phone book. Place another phone book on top for extra weight. Check them every couple of days for the first week to make sure they are not sticking to the paper.

In about three weeks, when they are completely dry, remove them to be used for a variety of crafts.

These containers take about an hour to make and cost about $12.

Materials & Tools

- Dried pressed ferns, leaves or flowers (one or two packages, or create homemade pressed plants)
- Set of two glass containers
- Decoupage medium
- Thin paintbrush
- Tweezers
- Bone folder or a wooden popsicle stick
- Cotton swabs
- Wax paper
- Tape

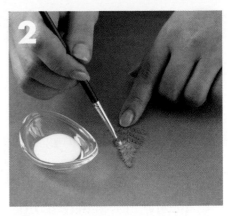

1 Tape a piece of wax paper to your work surface. This will protect the surface of your table when applying the decoupage medium to the pressed plants. Lay the pressed plant on top of the wax paper with the back side facing up. Gently brush a thin layer of decoupage medium to the back side of the plant. Let it dry slightly so it is not too wet — this makes it a little easier to apply to the glass. It is recommended to apply the decoupage medium to one pressed plant at a time.

3 After it has completely dried, apply several more layers of decoupage medium on top of each pressed plant. Allow each layer to completely dry before applying the next coat.

2 Use tweezers to help place the pressed plant onto the container. Wipe off any excess glue with a cotton swab. Then use a bone folder or a wooden popsicle stick to make sure the plant is smoothly applied to the surface.

Craft Tips

- Lay a towel underneath the glass container. This will help keep the container steady when applying the pressed plants onto the glass.

- Try using a clear decoupage spray after applying the pressed plants onto the containers. Flip the glass upside down and spray an even coat all over the container. This will ensure an even better seal for the pressed plants. It can also create a more uniform appearance to your final project.

GRANDPA'S BIRDHOUSE TABLE DECORATION

You know it's spring when you see the first robin, so bring spring to your table by adding a birdhouse as a centerpiece. Create a birdhouse with an open roof so that you can put newly blossomed daffodils and other spring flowers or plants inside the birdhouse. Decorate the birdhouse with cute welcome signs, Spanish moss, artificial birds and other fun bird-themed articles. To maintain the theme, add small birdhouse napkin rings for each table setting.

This simple pattern can be made by most crafters with simple tools and supplies. The pattern is cut from one 1- by 10-inch board and one 1- by 6-inch board. To keep it simple, the actual dimensions of the board are used as much as possible so that only straight line or 45-degree angle cuts are needed. The actual dimensions of a 1- by 10-inch board are $\frac{3}{4}$ by $9\frac{1}{4}$ inches. The dimensions of a 1- by 6-inch board are $\frac{3}{4}$ by $5\frac{1}{2}$ inches. These dimensions are used in the cutting directions to simplify the cutting. Since this birdhouse will only house flowers and plants, there is no need to adhere to special sizes that birds prefer.

This birdhouse can be cut, painted and assembled in an afternoon. The wood, dowel and nails can be purchased at most lumberyards for about $8 to $10. The paint, Spanish moss, artificial birds and other decorations can be purchased at most craft stores or the craft section of a variety store for about $5 or more, depending upon the embellishments selected.

Materials & Tools

- Handsaw or table saw
- Hammer
- Paintbrush
- Drill
- $\frac{1}{16}$-inch drill bit
- $\frac{1}{4}$-inch drill bit
- $1\frac{1}{2}$-inch hole saw bit
- One 1- by 10-inch pine board
- One 1- by 6-inch pine board
- Scraps of $\frac{1}{4}$-inch-thick wood
- One $\frac{1}{4}$- or $\frac{3}{8}$-inch wooden dowel
- Sanding paper
- Pencil
- Finishing nails
- Acrylic paint of choice (buttermilk, blue, green)
- Spanish moss
- Artificial birds
- Other decorations of choice

1 From the 1- by 10-inch pine board, cut one square measuring $9\frac{1}{4}$ by $9\frac{1}{4}$ inches for bottom of birdhouse. (To extend bottom to front of each birdhouse, cut bottom measuring $9\frac{1}{4}$ inches by $11\frac{1}{4}$ inches.)

Cut two birdhouse fronts with a house peak by drawing a rectangle $9\frac{1}{4}$ by $5\frac{1}{2}$ inches with pencil. Then draw a line exactly up the middle of the $9\frac{1}{4}$-inch section, at the $4\frac{5}{8}$-inch point. Put a hash mark 10 inches from base of front piece on middle line. This will be the peak of the birdhouse front.

Draw another line from top of the $5\frac{1}{2}$-inch corner to the 10-inch hash mark on middle line, and extend line to other side of board. Draw a line from top of other $5\frac{1}{2}$-inch corner to hash mark on middle line and extend line to other side of board. This will create the peak for the first front piece, and opposite it will be the peak for the second front piece.

Draw another rectangle beneath second opposite peak measuring $5\frac{1}{2}$ by $9\frac{1}{4}$ inches. Cut two front pieces on outer drawn lines using handsaw or table saw. Using hand drill and the $1\frac{1}{2}$-inch hole saw drill bit, drill a hole in the center of each of the two front pieces. Using drill and $\frac{1}{4}$-inch drill bit, drill a hole about $\frac{1}{2}$ inch below $1\frac{1}{2}$-inch hole, and about halfway through thickness of front board to place dowel for bird perch.

From the 1- by 6-inch board, cut two rectangles measuring 5½ by 7¾ inches with handsaw or table saw. These will be sides of birdhouse.

For roof pieces, from the 1- by 6-inch pine board, cut two pieces measuring 1½ by 5⅜ inches, two pieces measuring 1½ by 6¼ inches and two pieces measuring 1½ by 10¾ inches. Sand edges lightly with sanding paper. Wipe off excess dust with damp paper towel.

Using paintbrush or sponge brush, paint bottom green; paint front and side pieces buttermilk and roof pieces blue. Be sure to paint all sides that will be seen in assembled birdhouse. Dilute paint slightly with water to create a stain-like finish, or use paint full strength according to your preference. If necessary, apply a second coat of paint. Allow all pieces to dry.

2 Assemble house by nailing front pieces to side pieces with finishing nails. To prevent wood from splitting, drill pilot holes using an electric drill and 1/16-inch drill bit. Use two or three finishing nails for each side. Attach bottom to front and side pieces with finishing nails. Attach roof pieces to peak of house by nailing smallest piece in place first. Use only one nail for each piece to begin with, and add second nail after all pieces are in place to ensure a good fit of all pieces.

Align edge of roof piece with inside edge of house front so that the roof and inside edge of house front are flush on inside. Also align roof piece flush with peak of house. Remember to drill pilot holes with a drill before attaching the other smallest piece to opposite side of front peak. Nail medium-length piece of roof to other side of peak of each front. Align piece so it covers previous piece and is also flush with inside of house. Nail largest piece on each side of house. Align edge of largest piece so it is touching bottom of previous pieces. Make sure all pieces are flush with each other. Cut two pieces about 2 to 3 inches long from wooden dowel. Sand ends slightly with sanding paper. Push into holes drilled previously. Touch up paint if necessary.

3 Place planter with fresh spring plant inside house. Fall planted bulbs like daffodils, grape hyacinth or tulips can be planted indoors in early spring so they are ready to bloom and place in your birdhouse for your spring luncheon.

Or place container with a flower mold inside and arrange fresh or dried flowers in container. Create your own individual birdhouse by adding details that go with your home décor.

Using a hot-glue gun or double-back tape, adhere artificial bird to perch on each side of house. Put Spanish moss in hole of birdhouse on each side. If desired, additional flowers or designs can be painted on outside of house. Small signs with birdhouse-theme sayings can also be added.

Craft Tips

- To continue the birdhouse theme, add smaller versions of the birdhouse as napkin rings. The birdhouse napkin ring is created using scraps of wood remaining from birdhouse, making a smaller version of the "front piece" noted above. The hole in the birdhouse is big enough to pull a napkin halfway through. Select spring-colored napkins and place mats that match the floral centerpiece. If you selected fresh blooming bulbs, be sure to plant them outside after they are done blooming to continue the fun next spring.

- If you have a friend or family member with electric tools, the edge of the pattern pieces can be routed using a router before painting and assembling. Grandpa Gene is always helpful when a carpentry project is planned at our house.

- The birdhouse can also be used for other practical purposes: as a mailbox depository to keep your monthly bills and correspondence in one place or to hold cards and small gifts for a party or shower. Adjusting the measurements can easily make a taller version, which can sit on the floor and hold umbrellas or be used to display dried flowers, grasses and other garden decorations. Place one or two large red-twig dogwood branches into sand placed inside the container. Decorate the branches with small collectible birdhouses. You can also add other colorful objects to decorate for spring holidays, like green clover leaves for St. Patrick's Day or colorful eggs for Easter.

SPRING
GARDENING

S pring is for gardening, and gardening is for spring. Yes, you can spend time in your garden during the year's other seasons. But there's something magical about being outside when the air is clean, the soil is warm again and your hands are just itching to get a little dirty. So here are a variety of projects to help you add both flavor (in the form of vegetables and herbs) and color (in the form of both annual and perennial flowers) to your gardening endeavors.

Facing page: Rock Garden, page 143

WHAT TO GROW

Spring is time to start growing the vegetables you love to eat. This basic guide will help you make your plant selections.

When deciding what edibles to grow, be choosy and keep it simple. The more uncomplicated your plan, the less maintenance will be involved and the happier you will be with the results. The most important thing is to grow vegetables, fruits or herbs that you enjoy eating. And spring is the time to get started growing it all.

Here are some other questions to ask yourself as you choose what to grow. What is expensive to purchase at the market? What is hard to find? What is easy to find, but not of very good quality? The answers to those questions will guide your decisions. For instance, if all of your neighbors grow zucchini and are leaving bags full of zukes on your doorstep, then maybe zucchini shouldn't be tops on your list of things to plant.

Grocery List Gardening

If you plan your edible garden according to the growable items that turn up time and time again on your grocery list, your collection of vegetables and herbs will save you both time and money. Having things growing in your yard that you eat often makes sense in many ways. When you can go outside and pluck a few parsley stems when you need them, you throw out far fewer half-used bunches, and your parsley is fresher and prettier too. Also, our eating habits are just that, in that we tend to eat the same things over and over. So if your family regularly eats cucumbers or tomatoes or green onions,

Like many other members of the squash family, cucumber vines tend to produce bumper crops all at once, so you will probably want to keep plantings small.

you know the ones you grow will be appreciated, with little if any heartbreaking waste.

If your partner is the grocery shopper at your house, ask them to pass on their old lists for a few weeks. Old grocery lists are a

Lettuce is always a winning crop in a home garden. Leaf lettuces such as 'Oak Leaf' become crisp and sweet when they mature in cool weather.

Wondering Why
Growing Organic

Growing your own edibles organically is the perfect way to get pure, clean food not contaminated with chemicals. In a home garden, it just makes sense. You don't have to handle the toxic stuff and you don't have to eat produce laced with it. Besides, home gardens are naturally low-pest zones because of the diversity of plants grown there. In a mixed-up garden, pests are much less of a problem than they are in huge fields where only a single crop is grown. And if pests do become a nuisance, there are safe, earth-friendly alternatives to chemicals: insecticidal soap, baking soda, oil sprays and others.

All members of the cabbage family are outstanding vegetables to grow in climates where summers are cool. These include broccoli, cabbage, cauliflower and kohlrabi.

Plantings of sweet corn need to be large because there must be plenty of plants to share pollen.

gold mine of information on excellent edibles for your garden.

Climate and Quality

Your climate will influence the quality of the vegetables you grow, because most vegetables prefer either cool, warm or hot weather. You can work with these preferences by making use of seasonal weather changes, but you can push things only so far. Gardeners in cool climates will always have great luck with cool-natured vegetables such as lettuce and cabbage, while gardeners in hot climates often have pepper crops that zoom off the charts. Moderate climes often are home to the finest sweet corn and snap beans.

The beauty of well-grown vegetables is more than skin deep. When vegetables are so well matched to the climate and soil that they grow with ease, they often have slightly higher nutritional value too. In other words, happy vegetables in your garden are extra-healthy vegetables on your plate.

Getting into Varieties

Want more reasons to grow some of your own vegetables? If you spend a little time in the pages of seed catalogs (many of which are now on the Web), you'll quickly learn that there are dozens of variations in lettuce, and the same goes for squash, peppers, tomatoes and popular herbs like basil and mint. Some of the most remarkable varieties are never sold in grocery stores! So if you want to taste a yellow zucchini, roast some multicolored sweet corn or float a sprig of crinkled lemon mint in your tea, you may have to grow them yourself.

Sweet bell peppers need a long, warm season to ripen from green to their mature colors, which may be red, yellow or orange.

Irish potatoes are really from South America, where they are found in numerous colors and forms. Special seed potato companies make rare varieties available to gardeners.

SOW A SALAD GARDEN

You can grow your own salads! Actually, it's very easy when you follow this step-by-step plan. And the taste? Fresh and fabulous, of course!

Explore the endless variations in the color and texture of lettuce leaves in your garden. Front to back, here are butterhead, crisphead, red oak leaf and green oak leaf types.

Imagine the crunch of crispy lettuce and cucumbers, the tang of a fresh tomato, the bite of a green onion. Hungry yet? If you are, then you know that a salad of garden-fresh vegetables that you have grown yourself is beyond comparison.

You do not have to have a huge space or a lot of time to reap satisfying salad rewards. A single 3- by 6-foot bed can keep you in salad fixins for months. By using high-yielding vegetables and intensive planting techniques, you can harvest almost 50 pounds of produce from such small space! Here's how.

Build a Bed

A raised bed is perfect for a salad garden because it will provide the optimum growing conditions necessary for an intensively planted little patch. But any good, sunny spot will do.

Pick Your Plants

Let your palate be your guide in choosing what you would like to grow in your salad garden. Divide your bed into 6 squares of the same size (approximately 18 by 24 inches each). In each square, plug in a different salad veggie. The following are some suggestions for crops to start in spring, as well as ideas for what to plant in its space when it is finished. You may also want to plant edible flowers around the perimeter of the salad patch for pretty, and tasty, garnishes.

- Onions, followed by kale
- Sweet bell pepper
- Tomato, followed by spinach
- Radishes, followed by cucumbers, then lettuce or onions
- Spinach, followed by peppers
- Carrots
- Lettuce, followed by beets
- Lettuce, followed by chard

Try These
Flowers You Can Eat

Toss them in salads or use them as garnishes. These flowers taste as good as they look.

Lavender.

Nasturtiums

Squash blossoms

Pansies

Chives

Borage

Lavender

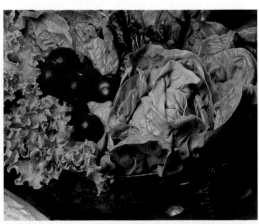

Spring lettuce is usually ready before tomatoes ripen, but you can have these two vegetables together by planting lettuce again when nights cool in late summer.

Try These
Cherry Tomatoes

The essence of summer in a bite-size package, cherry tomatoes are much closer to their "wild" relatives than their larger, meatier cousins. So they don't need pampering, and they are top choices for a less-work garden. First, forget staking, trellising or tying this baby to a pole. It's like roping the wind, and nothing will frustrate you more than a cherry tomato that's been fenced in and is trying desperately to break out. Instead, position cherry tomato plants at the edge of the garden where they can be allowed free rein. Cherry tomatoes make an attractive cascading border for the garden, or even a fun barrel planting. Don't worry when overripe fruits fall to the ground. Let them rot there, and you will never have to buy a cherry tomato plant again because hundreds of volunteer plants will sprout up next year and every year thereafter. Weed out the seedlings you don't want, and allow a few keepers to grow.

Sprightly cherry tomatoes come in a range of sizes and colors, from tiny red or yellow 'currant' varieties to meatier small globes such as red 'Sweet Chelsea.'

Ease Through the Seasons

To push cool-loving salad crops like lettuce and spinach into summer, shield them with some shade cloth. Available at most garden centers, the fabric covering allows just enough light to pass through to promote healthy growth, while filtering out the sun's strongest rays. You may also consider planting a summer salad garden in a lightly shaded area, or let some lettuces grow in the shade of taller plants such as tomatoes.

You can replace fast-growing radishes and greens with cucumbers, chard or heat-loving peppers. Divide your bed into sections to make replanting easy.

remove it and get the next crop in the ground. By never letting the bed go idle, you can reap big yields from such a small space.

Keep It Working

By planting a salad garden in a compact area, it will be easy to tend. Keep your crops well watered to promote robust growth. Weeding should be a snap. Because plants are spaced so closely, weeds will have a hard time getting a foothold. Any that do sprout will be easy to see and remove. Harvest crops as soon as they are ready and as often as possible. This will encourage the vegetables to produce more. As soon as one vegetable is finished,

Garden Tip
When to Plant

Vegetable	Planting Time
Beets	Spring, midsummer
Carrots	Spring
Chard	Spring, midsummer
Cucumbers	Late spring
Kale	Midsummer
Lettuce	Spring, midsummer, late summer
Onions	Spring, late summer
Peppers	Late spring
Radishes	Spring
Spinach	Spring, midsummer
Tomatoes	Late spring

Carrots.

Radishes.

A Salsa Garden

Don't settle for store-bought salsa. Grow your own!

Peppers give salsa both color and flavor. Most hot peppers are green, but sweet peppers in pretty colors are great to use in salsas that include fresh fruit.

Fill a small garden bed with flavor and send your tastebuds on a culinary tour south of the border by growing the essential ingredients for salsa! In a space no bigger than 2 by 5 feet, you can grow all the peppers, tomatoes, onions, tomatillos and cilantro that you'll need to make loads of salsa for you and your friends. And you will probably have enough produce left over for other culinary adventures as well.

The fundamentals for salsa making are fairly basic. At a minimum, you'll only need one plant each of peppers, tomatoes and tomatillos. You'll also need several onions and a few cilantro plants.

Peppers

Anything goes when it comes to peppers suitable for salsa. For most aficionados, the hotter, the better! Jalapeño peppers are a standard for salsa, with their excellent not-too-hot spicy flavor. If you prefer, there are even jalapeño varieties available that are barely hot, so you can enjoy their flavor without as much of the bite. Moving up into more fiery peppers there are 2-inch long, fleshy serrano peppers and heart-shaped, 3- to 5-inch-long ancho peppers. Then there's the habanero—one of the hottest peppers you can grow. If hot isn't your thing, you can grow a bell pepper or two for adding succulent sweetness to a

Habanero peppers are easy to grow yet too hot for most people to eat. Be sure to wear gloves when handling hot peppers like these.

Wondering Why
Peppers Heat Up in Hot Weather

A compound called capsaicin gives hot peppers their fire. And when it gets hotter outside, your hot peppers get hotter inside. Why? Because stress on the plant makes them turn up the heat. Stress can come in many forms—too little water, not enough nutrients—but the stress most likely to make peppers more fiery is nighttime temperatures. Hot nights stress plants the most and make for hotter peppers. That explains why a pepper grown in one region can be so much hotter than the same variety grown during the same season in a cooler climate.

Anaheim peppers are packed with flavor but usually have very little heat. They make a rich, full-flavored salsa.

tame salsa. Plant one pepper plant per square foot of garden bed.

When onion tops fall over, they are ready to pull. To cure, lay them out to dry for a week or more. But you can eat uncured onions, which are often extra sweet and juicy.

Onions

The easiest way to grow the onions necessary for great salsa is to plunk a few onion sets (little baby onion bulbs) in the ground in spring. Take your pick from white, yellow or red—any of them will work well. Plant about 16 sets per square foot to get good-sized bulbs.

Tomatoes

If you only plan on growing one tomato plant, then choose one that will not only make delicious salsa but will also provide great fruits for slicing and otherwise enjoying. That means picking a beefsteak-type tomato with large, juicy, flavorful fruits. If you have the room to grow two tomato plants in your salsa garden, then add an egg-shaped paste tomato. The smaller, meatier fruits will lend a thicker consistency to your condiment endeavors. If you are staking or caging your tomato plant, then place one plant per square foot.

You can use the same tomatoes for salsa that you use for salads and sandwiches. Peel, chop, and you're ready to make salsa.

Tomatillos

These sweet-tart fruits are the secret of the green version of salsa. The tomatillo is actually a relative of the tomato, and requires the same kind of care. In fact, tomatillo means "little tomato." The glossy, firm fruits are clothed in a papery husk. Pick when the husks have just turned from green to buff, but while the fruits are still green. Give this plant at least 2 square feet (or more) to ramble; expect a few volunteers to spring up next year.

Tomatillo plants are tall and rangy, and they produce huge crops in warm summer weather. They can also reseed wildly, so gather up fallen fruits when you spot them.

Cilantro

Salsa gets its pungently full flavor from the leaves of this herb. Cilantro is very easy to grow from seed and likes cool weather. It will bloom and make seed in no time flat (its seeds are actually the well-known spice, coriander), so sow successive plantings to get enough leaves for all your salsa ventures.

Care and Harvest

Keep your plants well watered through summer so they keep pumping out the ingredients for the hot stuff. Harvest any ripe produce regularly so the plants continue to produce. If you have staked the tomato plant, continue to tie it to the stake as it grows. Pull onions as needed before their tops brown. When their tops brown, pull all of them and allow them to dry in a cool, dry place for several days before storing them.

Recipe
Salsa

10 lbs. roma tomatoes, peeled and cut into desired size

1 jar sliced jalapeño peppers, finely chopped

10 to 20 assorted hot and sweet peppers (mild, medium or hot), finely chopped

6 limes, peeled, squeezed (juice and pulp reserved)

4 garlic cloves, mashed

1 bunch cilantro, stems removed, finely chopped

3 large red onions, finely chopped

3 large yellow onions, finely chopped

1 cup granulated sugar

¼ cup salt

1 tablespoon freshly ground pepper

1 In large pot, combine tomatoes, peppers, limes, garlic, cilantro, onions, sugar, salt and pepper; cook over medium heat 30 minutes.

2 Pour salsa evenly into clean jars for canning. Follow standard canning practices. Refrigerate or eat immediately. Or, for great intensity of flavor, do not cook — eat raw!

Matt Dillon
Roanoke, Virginia

A KITCHEN HERB GARDEN

There's nothing like snipping a few fresh herbs outside your kitchen door!

Culinary herbs including rosemary, sage, thyme and chervil share bed space with coral sage and nasturtiums. The potted rosemary can be brought indoors in winter.

Garden Tip
Keep Mint in Bounds

Mint is a great herb, but it may actually grow too well and crowd out every other herb in the garden if you don't take precautionary measures. The easiest way to keep mint in bounds is to cut out the bottom of a large plastic pot, then dig a hole so the pot can be sunk all the way up to its rim. Fill the area inside the pot with soil, and set your mint plant within the boundary the pot provides. The pot will provide a barrier to creeping underground roots—the key to managing mint.

A half whiskey barrel holds a refreshing crop of mint. Mint strains vary in their appearance and flavor.

You can combine the herbs to create a small bed that is as attractive as it is useful. Site the bed in full sun close to your house, so herbs can be harvested quickly and easily as needed. The bed design here is triangular, perfect for tucking into a corner where a walkway, patio or fence meets the house. This planting pattern can be adapted to beds of different shapes and sizes too.

Planting the Patch

Begin your herb garden in winter by ordering seeds and plants from mail-order or online purveyors. They will send plants to you at the perfect time for planting in your area. If you choose to wait until spring to get started,

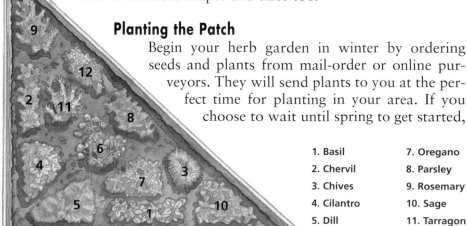

1. Basil	7. Oregano
2. Chervil	8. Parsley
3. Chives	9. Rosemary
4. Cilantro	10. Sage
5. Dill	11. Tarragon
6. Lovage	12. Thyme

the herbs in this design can be easily found at garden centers or nurseries.

Prepare the site for the herb garden by outlining the bed on the ground with string or a line of lime or flour. Remove any grass. Be sure the soil is dry enough to work and, using a spading fork, loosen the soil to a depth of about 8 inches. Spread a 1- to 2-inch layer of compost over the bed and dig it into the soil. Rake the soil surface smooth.

Following the planting diagram, start planting in spring. Sow seeds of dill, cilantro and chervil first. Water lightly each day until seedlings appear. Set out herb plants in spring. Wait until after your last frost to plant rosemary or basil.

All-Weather Access

Nothing beats the convenience of an herb garden in the backyard. But did you ever dash out to grab a few sprigs of thyme for that perfect chicken dish in November, only to waste time mopping up all the mud you tracked into the house from your quick jaunt to the herb patch? Consider providing all-weather access to your herb garden by making walkways that won't turn to mud!

You may want to lay permanent steppingstones or spread a thick layer of gravel in the path. Either approach will complement the informal nature of an herb garden. If you do not want to install a permanent path, or if it is too late in the year to do so, simply plop down a few wide planks to provide safe, clean footing as you harvest in less-than-perfect weather.

Caring for the Herbs

Mulch around your herbs to reduce weeding chores and keep the soil moist. Mulch will also reduce the need to water. Start harvesting herbs a month or so after planting by pinching or snipping off leaves. Seed heads of cilantro and dill are ready to harvest when they darken in color. Snip the seed heads off and put them in a paper bag to catch the seeds as they finish drying.

Try These
Annual, Perennial or Biennial?

The life span of an herb can be discerned by whether it is called an annual, perennial or biennial. Annuals, such as basil and dill, grow and die in one season. You may need to get more seed or plants of these each year. Perennials (such as oregano) keep coming back year after year. Biennials (such as parsley) will grow leaves the first year, and then go to seed and die during the second year. Oftentimes, biennials are treated like annuals and replaced each year.

An annual, basil craves warm weather and quickly produces flowers and seeds. Pinch plants back to keep them leafy.

A biennial, parsley flowers and sets seed in its second year. Plant new seedlings each spring and fall.

A perennial, oregano dies back to the ground in winter. It rebounds first thing in spring.

PLUG-IN VEGGIES

Don't wait for seeds to grow. Get a head start with plug-in veggies.

Vegetable seedlings grown in containers will quickly take off in your garden—provided they have received regular water and plenty of light.

Try These
Best Bets for Spring

Cantaloupe

Cucumbers

Eggplant

Hot peppers

Squash

Sweet peppers

Tomatoes

Watermelon

Plant edibles from this list early enough in spring so that they can take full advantage of late spring's and early summer's lengthening days; that's when these plants will grow like mad. Shown: cantaloupe.

In these days of hectic lifestyles, it's not uncommon that weeks slip by and you haven't had a chance to think about a garden, let alone plant one. But even if you think the prime planting time has passed away, don't write off having a garden until next year. It's never too late to start a garden if you choose the right vegetables to grow for the season you're in.

And it won't take very long to whip a garden together, either. With all the transplants available at garden centers, you can have a respectable garden planted in a weekend, with very little effort. As an added bonus for procrastinating, you will probably find that many transplants go on sale at bargain-basement prices after spring garden-fever subsides. So what are you waiting for? Time's a-wasting if you want a red, ripe and juicy tomato or sweet, crunchy carrots!

Dig In

Before you head out to purchase transplants, assess your garden site. That way, you'll know exactly what you need and what will fit, so you won't over-buy.

Do any preparation necessary to get the garden ready for planting ahead of time, so when you get home with your new transplants, all you have to do is "plug and play." Remove any dead plants from last year, and hoe or till any weeds that have begun to grow this year. If you do not plan to till, loosen up the soil with a spading fork. Rake the soil level and form beds, if you desire. Get the sprinkler in place.

If you will not be planting for a day or two and the weather has been dry, go ahead and turn the sprinkler on for a little while to soak the ground. If you are going to be planting the same day you get the garden ready, then wait until after you plant to turn on the sprinkler.

Shop Smart

Take a trip to at least two local garden centers or nurseries. There, you'll probably be able to find plants that haven't been neglected too much even though the buying rush is over. Look for plants that are vibrant-green and as compact as possible. Avoid anything that's wilted, brown or otherwise sickly looking.

If you purchase any plants that have fruits on them, such as tomatoes or peppers, pinch off the fruits before you plant. That way the plants will devote more energy into sending out roots rather than developing fruits.

While you're shopping, consider picking up some bedding plants of annual flowers. They will help to dress up your veggie patch and provide a little excitement for the eyes while you wait for the vegetable plants to fill in.

Planting Pleasure

Planting a plug-in garden is a breeze. All you need is a good trowel, and away you go. Simply dig holes, and pop plants in where you want them. That's it!

One advantage to planting a garden in a weekend is that you can develop an overall design scheme with the actual plants rather than guessing what will go where as the season progresses. Snip the six-packs apart so you have individual plants in individual little pots. Arrange your plants until you get the best layout; the little pots will prevent their tender roots from getting dried out. Be creative in your design—vegetable gardens do not require soldier-straight rows with all the same things in rows all by themselves. Mix and mingle the plants for a visually interesting garden that naturally resists pest attacks. Intermingled plantings confuse pest insects, so it's harder for them to find a meal.

Keep plant spacing in mind. Remember that the darling little 6-inch-tall tomato transplant is going to grow into a 4-foot-tall behemoth in short order. Imagine what each vegetable will look like full grown, and space accordingly. Remember to position plants so it is easy to tend them too. Give rambling plants like cucumbers a place near the garden's edge, where they can wander without being stepped on when you're trying to weed.

Garden Tip
Planting Leggy Tomatoes

When picking up tomato transplants at the garden center, you're bound to run into plants that have grown tall and spindly because they've been kept in a container for too long. These oldsters are fine to plant in the garden if you follow this advice. Pinch off all the lower branches, leaving only the top two or three. Then dig a deep hole or a horizontal trench, and bury that tomato plant all the way up to the top leaves. The plant will quickly form roots all along the buried stem, making a much stronger plant that you will not have to coddle!

The lowest section of a tomato's main stem will quickly sprout roots if it is buried in damp soil. This will lead to a more vigorous and productive plant.

GROWING ANNUALS FROM SEED

If you start them early and indoors, your annuals will produce color in the garden that much faster, once you set them out. Here are the secrets to successfully starting annuals from seed.

It's so fun to get a head start on spring by starting seeds indoors. Many interesting annuals are hard to find as bedding plants, or you may want to grow a dozen or more plants in a particular color. But seed starting is not limited to spring. In summer and fall, you can gear up for the "second season" by starting ornamental kale, pansies, foxglove, and other hardy

Make up your own planting mix or use potting soil straight from the bag. Be sure to mix materials together well before filling pots or seedling containers.

Seeds will be more likely to stay at the proper planting depth if you moisten the planting medium before sowing seeds. Lay seeds on the surface and then push them into the mixture with a stick or pencil.

plants indoors. On hot summer days, seeded containers kept outdoors can be impossible to keep moist.

Turning a tabletop into a seedling nursery is easily done with the help of suitable containers, growing medium, and supplemental light. For containers, simply clean and reuse the cellpacks commercial growers use to grow bedding plants. Other good seedling containers include peat pots, small plastic cups with drainage holes punched in the bottoms, or deep trays saved from fresh produce or convenience foods. Or, you can sow entire flats with seeds if you want to grow a large number of the same plant. All containers used to grow seedlings should be at least 2 inches deep to accommodate the plants' fast-growing roots. They must have drainage holes too.

What you put in the containers is more important than the containers themselves. Potting soils used for starting seeds are not really soils at all and are more properly described as soil-less mixes. In place of soil, these products are made up primarily of either milled

After seeds are planted, use a fine mist of water to keep the soil's surface slightly moist at all times. Avoid a strong stream of water, which may make the seeds float toward the surface.

Annual flower seeds come in many shapes and sizes. Counterclockwise starting from bottom right, note the differences between impatiens, bachelor button, snapdragon, nasturtium, zinnia, sweet alyssum, pansy, and marigold and cosmos in the center. Very small seeds are often coated to make them easier to handle, as has been done here with the snapdragon seeds.

sphagnum peat moss or vermiculite—both very fine, soft-textured substances that will not form a crust over emerging seeds. Labels vary from one product to another, but most bags of soil-less mix do claim to be great for starting seeds.

Before planting seeds, fill containers to the top with soil-less mix and dampen them thoroughly. Prepare markers that will identify the flowers you are planting, and get ready to sow.

Conditioning Seeds

Most seeds of annual flowers can be planted in moist soil-less mix straight from the packet, but some need special treatment to help them germinate. Some gardeners like to refrigerate all flower seeds for a few days before sowing them. Chilling is most beneficial to cool-season plants that are sown while the weather is warm, such as foxglove, pansy, and ornamental cabbage and kale, but it will not hurt any flower seeds. The logic

behind this practice is that chilling gives the seeds the impression that winter has suddenly turned to spring, the season for sprouting.

Large, hard seeds such as abelmoschus, hyacinth bean, sweet peas and nasturtiums will germinate faster if you soak them overnight in warm water before

Large seeds with hard seedcoats benefit from being soaked in warm water overnight before planting.

planting them. Place the seeds you want to plant in a clean container, cover with an inch or more of warm water, and allow them to sit at room temperature until the next day.

Some seeds that have very hard seedcoats sprout much faster if you nick the dry seeds with a sharp knife or abrade them with a steel file. The objective of this process, called scarification, is to make deep scratches

Some seeds have such thick coats that they absorb moisture better if they are abraded with a knife, steel file or coarse sandpaper. This is called scarification.

in the seedcoat. These scratches help the seeds soak up water and make it easier for the seed to break open when the sprout is ready to emerge. Some annual seeds that benefit from scarification include cup and saucer vine, moonvine and morning glory.

To keep seeded containers constantly moist, enclosed them loosely in a plastic bag or cover the surface with a piece of plastic. Remove the covers as soon as the first seeds sprout.

If you tend to lose track of time, use an automatic timer to turn your plant lights on and off. Stretched out, leggy growth is a sign that seedlings need more light.

Planting Depth

The standard guideline for seed planting, which is to bury seeds about three times as deep as the seed is wide, will serve you well with most flower seeds that are larger than a pinhead. But the seeds of many annuals are smaller than this, and the smaller the seed, the more likely it is to respond well to surface planting.

Planting tiny seeds by barely pressing them into the surface of containers filled with moist soilless mix has two advantages. First, the seeds are exposed to light, and light acts as a germination trigger for some species. And later, when the seeds germinate, they are in no danger of being buried so deeply that the sprouts face a difficult struggle making it through a cover of soil to life-giving light.

To keep surface-sown seeds constantly moist, commercial growers use elaborate mist systems that moisten such seeds several times a day. For gardeners, it's more practical to enclose planted containers in loose plastic bags until the first green sprouts appear.

Some of the more challenging annual seeds need shallow or surface sowing and dark conditions to germinate well. For these flowers, enclose the planted containers in a brown paper bag or place them in a dark cabinet or closet for a few days. Check them often after the fourth day, because you will need to move them to good light promptly after germination begins.

Promoting Strong Germination

To simulate the brightness of the sun, buy a fluorescent grow light that can be suspended above the plants and kept on 10 to 12 hours a day. Ideally, the light should be adjustable so you can keep it about 2 inches higher

When the roots of seedlings are kept warm, they often grow faster and stronger. If you use a heating cable or other heat source for this purpose, turn it on during the day and off at night.

than the tops of the plants. Special bulbs made for growing plants emit a very intense spectrum of light, but they do cost more than standard bulbs. You can save money by building your own fixture and buying the bulbs separately. An inexpensive automatic timer is also a good investment, especially if you are often away from home.

Besides helping seedlings grow, the light will provide a little supplemental heat. Young seedlings often grow faster if their roots are kept a few degrees warmer than room temperature. Special heating cables are sold to provide bottom heat to seeded flats, or you can rig up your own using a small heating pad set on its lowest setting. But instead of placing damp containers directly on a heating pad, set two short wood boards on bricks or books, slide the heating pad into the space below the boards, and place your seedlings on the boards.

How To
Pricking Out

1 Lifting or squeezing from the bottom, remove the clump of seedlings from their container.

2 Lay the clump on its side and tap the roots gently

3 Pick up a seedling by gently grasping a seedling leaf. Do not touch the main stem or roots except to give them gentle support.

4 Gently replant seedling into a new container filled with lightly dampened soil-less mix. Water well. Protect the replanted seedlings from strong light for 2 days.

After seedlings show shapely true leaves, begin fertilizing with a water-soluble fertilizer mixed at half strength. Water the soil rather than the leaves, which are best kept dry.

Thinning and Transplanting

Frequently, more seeds will sprout than should be allowed to grow in a small container. To ease crowding, use tweezers to pull out all but two seedlings in each 2-inch-wide container. You also can use cuticle scissors to clip off unwanted seedlings at the soil line.

If you have planted a mixture of colors of a certain annual, be careful not to thin out only the smallest seedlings. Flower color is often associated with seedling vigor in annual flowers, so it's important to thin out an even distribution of small-, medium-, and large-sized seedlings to make sure you end up with a nice mix of colors.

You also can replant crowded seedlings as soon as they show their first true leaf. This process, called pricking out, calls for patience and steady hands, but it is not difficult to do.

Fertilizing Seedlings

Seeds contain sufficient nutrients to energize newly germinated seedlings, but because soil-less mixes contain little, if any, plant food, it's important to start feeding your seedlings as soon as they show one true leaf. The simplest method is to use a soluble fertilizer mixed with water at half the rate recommended on the label. Many organic gardeners use fish emulsion fertilizer for this purpose, but other water-soluble fertilizers work well too. For best results, mix a small amount of fertilizer with the water each time you moisten the soil. To avoid spilling, use a squeeze bottle to deliver "rich water" to your seedlings. Wait until you set your plants out to switch to a more convenient granular or powdered plant food.

Until weather conditions are right for planting, keep seedlings in a cold frame or other protected place. Remove covers on bright sunny days to let excess heat escape.

Hardening Off

Whether you grow your own seedlings or adopt them in six-packs, the process of moving young plants outdoors is best done gradually over a period of about 2 weeks. This process, called hardening off, helps stems to toughen, lets leaves become accustomed to the effects of full-strength sun, and forces roots to adapt to fluctuating day and night temperatures. You do not need to wait until your home-grown seedlings are as large as those sold as bedding plants to harden them off. As indoor growing space becomes crowded, it's fine to start hardening off your most cold hardy seedlings when they have as few as 4 to 6 leaves. After hardening off, you can keep them in a protected place outdoors until you are ready to plant them.

The classic way to harden off seedlings is to use a cold frame, which is basically a wood box with a glass or translucent lid, set on the ground. However, any place where the seedlings will get good light and be protected from strong winds will do, including plastic-covered tunnels, an enclosure made from bales of hay, or near a warm south-facing wall of your house.

The important thing is to harden off seedlings gradually. Leave them outdoors for only an hour or two the first day, then a half day, and finally all day by the end of the first week. The second week, allow seedlings to stay outdoors day and night unless the weather is very cold or windy. By this time, the plants should be tough enough to transplant whenever you are ready.

Direct Seeding Your Herbs

Annuals with fragile or brittle roots such as poppies and larkspur are so easily damaged that the gentlest of transplanting operations leaves them weak. The solution is to sow the seeds where the plants are to grow. You can also direct-sow bachelor buttons, nasturtiums, sunflowers, zinnias and many other annuals to save time and unnecessary trouble. Among annual flowers, most of the best candidates for

In loose, porous soil, direct seeding is a simple matter of placing seeds in a shallow furrow and covering them up. Plant twice as many seeds as you really need, and thin them to proper spacing a few weeks later. It's much better to have too many seedlings than too few.

Try These

Here are the best times to plant annuals that grow well when direct-seeded:

- **Late Winter:** Hardy annuals including bachelor button, larkspur, poppies and sweet peas. In mild winter areas, these flowers can be planted in the fall.

- **Early Spring:** Cool-season annuals such as ammi, bells of Ireland, black-eyed Susan, calendula, cosmos, gaillardia and sweet alyssum.

- **Mid-Spring to Early Summer:** Tender annuals like abelmoschus, coreopsis, hyacinth bean, lavatera, marigold, melampodium, Mexican suflower, morning glory, sunflower, touch-me-not and zinnia.

Bachelor button seedlings withstand cold weather, so they can be planted in fall in many areas. They reseed well, too, and the seeds are goldfinch favorites.

Cosmos are such energetic germinators that there is little point in starting them in containers. Simply sow them where you want them to grow from early spring to early summer.

Direct-seed zinnias where you want them to grow, and look for plenty of volunteer plants in subsequent seasons. Should you find yourself with too many seedlings, they are easy to dig and move.

direct seedling have medium- to large-sized seeds.

Direct seeding is simple if you have soft, loamy soil, but it can be a challenge if your soil type is clay. Because clay soil often forms a hard crust over germinating seeds, it is best to first blanket the planting site with an inch of compost or peaty potting soil—the next best thing to starting seeds indoors. Plant seeds directly into this medium and keep them constantly moist. For the first 3 to 4 days after planting, you can place an old blanket or boards over the seeded site to help keep the soil damp at all times. Remove the cover at the first sign that green sprouts are trying to push themselves through to the surface.

Until you learn what various seedlings look like, sow seed in a recognizable pattern such as parallel lines, zigzags or overlapping circles. Unless heavy rain rearranges the placement of the seeds, the pattern will make it easy to distinguish between flower seedlings and weeds.

If too many seedlings appear, thin them to proper spacing gradually. Should some seedlings pop up in odd places, you can move them by using a tablespoon to lift both the seedling and the ball of soil beneath it. Slip the little plant into its new site without shattering the root ball, and water well. As extra insurance, it's a good idea to shade transplanted seedlings with a small box or upside-down flowerpot for a day or two after they are moved.

To thin crowded seedlings, pull them out, roots and all. Use tweezers if needed to thin closely spaced plants. If the roots of adjoining plants become damaged as you thin, use sharp scissors to cut off the unwanted ones at the soil line.

Working with Bedding Plants

There's much more to working with bedding plants than just sticking them in the ground.

Bedding plants that already show a bloom or two make it easy to choose colors that you find appealing. Select plants that appear young and vigorous, and set them out as promptly as possible.

In gardening, few things are as simple as picking up a cellpack or two of bedding plants and popping them into the ground. The greenhouse growers who raise the plants control temperature, light and fertilizer very closely to produce high-quality plants that grow vigorously once you set them free in your garden.

Should you buy large plants or small ones? Those already in bloom or others just showing their first buds? Although most shoppers choose plants already in flower, bedding plants that have already produced several blooms are less desirable because of their advanced age. Confined to a small cellpack, many annuals are held back by matted, compacted roots if they wait too long on the shelf.

However, bedding plants showing their first one or two blooms are perfectly adoptable if you remedy their root problems right away. To do this, turn the plant upside down, squeeze the roots out of the container, and use your fingers to tease apart the bottom third of the root mass. Frequently you will need to break some roots to spread them, but this is necessary violence. Left in a tight spiral, the roots may never spread out into surrounding soil, which results in skimpy, short-lived plants.

After transplanting to larger pots or to the garden, pinch off any old blossoms as well as stems that may have been twisted or broken. Then thoroughly soak the plants. In very bright sunny weather, it's a good idea to shade plants for a few days after setting them out, especially if they have lost a fair number of roots.

Gently loosen the roots of seedlings after you remove them from containers, and spread those roots out as you set the plants in the soil. This helps plants develop the extensive root systems needed to support strong flowering.

If seedlings are too tall and leggy, pinch them back after transplanting. Within a few weeks, they will develop new stems that are stronger and stockier than the ones you removed.

Combining bedding plants into a container bouquet is easy and fun. In containers, choose colors and textures the same way you would if you were arranging annuals in an outdoor bed.

PROPAGATING CUTTINGS

It's fun and easy to grow plants from cuttings.

Coleus is the easiest annual to propagate from stem cuttings. Cuttings are so willing to develop roots that they will do so when kept in plain water.

Growing new plants by rooting stem cuttings is fun, and it's much easier with some annuals than with others. The best candidates for vegetative propagation include coleus, geranium, impatiens, lantana, Persian shield and ornamental sweet potato. If you are careful (and lucky), you can also root stem cuttings of bacopa, wax begonia, browallia, dusty miller, fan flower, fuchsia, heliotrope and mimulus.

Smart Sticking

Stem cuttings root best in a warm, humid environment where there is good light, but out of strong sun. You can "stick" cuttings indoors, or work outdoors in a shady, sheltered spot. The most versatile rooting medium is a half-and-half mixture of peat moss and clean sand, but you can also use perlite, vermiculite, or sterile soil-less mix. Whatever medium you choose must be kept constantly moist.

Use a sharp knife to take 4-inch-long cuttings from stem tips that do not have flowers. Pinch off all of the leaves except the cluster on the tip of the stem, dip the end in rooting powder (sold at nurseries and garden centers), and "stick" the cutting 3 inches deep in a container or bed filled with rooting medium. Cover the cuttings with light-colored cloth if needed to protect them from strong sun. With luck, the cuttings will grow roots and be ready to transplant in about a month. To check to see if a cutting is ready, pull on it gently. Cuttings with roots will resist a moderate tug.

When rooting stem cuttings, keep in mind that not every cutting will "take." To allow for failure, set a few more cuttings to root than you actually plan to use.

Try These
Double Pot Propagation

Here is a tried- and true-method for rooting stem cuttings indoors in a bright room. Fill a large unglazed clay flowerpot half full of rooting medium. Plug the hole in the bottom of a small unglazed pot, and place it in the center of the larger one. Fill the space between the two pots with rooting medium, and dampen thoroughly. Fill the small pot with water, and set cuttings to root in the space between the pots.

Moisture from the small pot will keep the medium moist. If desired, erect a plastic tent over the cuttings to help maintain high humidity—an easy way to ensure a high rate of rooting success. Once the cuttings have rooted, lift and transplant them the same way you would handle seedlings grown from seed.

To prepare a stem cutting for rooting, clip off blooms and buds along with all but 2 or 3 leaves near the tip. When roots develop, new stems should grow from the topmost nodes on the cutting.

SUPPORTING YOUR PLANTS

Some plants need extra support. Here's how to provide it.

All annual vines need a trellis on which to grow, and several tall flowers need to be staked or otherwise supported to help them stay upright. Plan ahead when you grow an annual that you know will need support, and install trellises or stakes at planting time if you can. Be as creative as you like when choosing support strategies for your annuals, and tailor your approach to the special needs of the plants.

Vertical Trellises for Vines

Because annual vines are short-lived plants, temporary trellises that can be put up or taken down quickly are best. Whenever it seems practical, see if you can find a way to weave a trellis with jute or lightweight cotton string. At the end of the season, you can cut down the string and the vine in one fell swoop and toss the whole thing in your compost heap. This saves you the tedious job of picking dead stems and tendrils from wire, chainlink fencing or polyester netting.

When you use an annual vine as a free-standing upright feature in a bed, a teepee made of bamboo or wood is hard to beat. By design, a teepee-shaped trellis stands up well since the weight of the vine pushes in upon itself. Twining vines that twist around their support (asarina, black-eyed Susan vine, hyacinth bean, moonvine, morning glory) will run right up a teepee trellis, but to please the delicate tendrils of sweet peas you'll need to weave string horizontally between the stakes.

Staking Tall Flowers

As tall flowers come into bloom, the briefest of summer showers can cause them to list badly or to fall over entirely. Usually a combination of factors is involved: The flowers become heavy with rainwater, the soil softens, making it easy for roots to slide about, and then a gust of wind comes along and pushes the plant over.

When this happens to foxgloves, hollyhock, Mexican sunflower and sunflower, the plants continue to bloom as best they can, but not with the grandeur of upright plants. Stake these annuals by pushing thin bamboo stakes into the ground that are as high as you think the plant will grow. Use twist ties to secure the main bud-bearing stems to the stake at 12-inch intervals.

Morning glories and other twining vines do well on any firm type of trellis made of wood, wire or even chainlink fence.

Garden Tip
Horizontal Support for Lanky Plants

To keep cosmos, dahlia, lisianthus, large-flowered marigold, snapdragon, stocks and tall zinnias upright, let their main stems grow up through a wire arch, wire support hoops or a matrix of string woven between secure stakes. For best results, the horizontal trellis should be about 15 inches above the ground.

Support bushy plants that are prone to toppling over, such as tall snapdragons, with stakes and string. By the time the plants reach full size, foliage and flowers will hide the support structure from view.

GROOMING YOUR FLOWERS

Once spring flowers start blooming, you have to take care of them.

Pinching off dead blossoms, called deadheading, is a crucial step for keeping annuals in bloom for the longest possible time. Pinch off tender stems with your fingers. You may need pruning shears for bigger jobs.

Some annual flowers are called "self-cleaning" because they do such a neat job of shedding their spent flowers. Impatiens and vinca are famous for this talent, which makes easy work of keeping the plants looking neat and well groomed. Ammi, larkspur, sunflower and other annuals that bloom all at once also require little upkeep, but many long-blooming species benefit from deadheading or shearing back.

Deadheading

An annual flower's prime purpose in life is to produce seeds. So, when you come along with a sharp pair of pruning shears and nip off blossoms as soon as they lose their looks, the frustrated plant has no choice but to respond by making more flowers. Because deadheading (garden lingo for trimming off old flowers) stops the seed-making process in its tracks, it's a fundamental way to make annuals bloom as long and strong as possible.

When deadheading, cut stems off just above a place where it looks like a new bud-bearing stem is poised to emerge. These growing points, called nodes, quickly grow into leafy new stems. With plants that bear on spikes, you need not wait until the last blossom on the spike has opened. Instead, cut them off when the bottom half of the spike has begun to wither. If you clean off the spent blossoms, the rest of the spike may still be useful as a cut flower.

Shearing Back

It's not practical to deadhead species that produce hundreds of bud-bearing stems such as lobelia, nierembergia, or sweet alyssum. Instead, use hedge clippers, sheep shears or a large pair of scissors to cut the plants back by about half their size in mid-summer. This process, called shearing back, is also used to stimulate new growth of tired browallia, fan flower and petunia being grown in hanging baskets. After shearing back any annual flower, follow up with a fresh application of fertilizer and a deep drench of water.

Just as with most other plants, new stems emerge from growing points along the stems of annual flowers, called nodes. Overgrown annuals will make a quick comeback if you prune stems to just above a healthy node.

To promote the growth of new flowering stems on lobelia and other small-flowered annuals, shear them back by one-third their size in mid-summer, after a very heavy flush of flowers leaves them looking slightly ragged.

QUICK COLOR FROM SIX-PACKS

Adding garden color is fast and easy when you use six-packs of annuals.

If you want to work up a good case of spring fever, visit a garden center in the spring and get lost in the sea of bedding plants offered for sale. It won't take long to conjure up dreamy visions of summer flowers dancing in your yard, and few things are simpler than growing flowers from bedding plants. But even if you grow only the toughest of bedding plants, such as begonias or pansies, skipping bed preparation or neglecting basic maintenance can spell trouble. To make sure your summer flowers thrive with little care, it's important to shop carefully, plant right and give your garden thoughtful care.

In the interest of reduced maintenance, keep your collection small, and try to create concentrated splashes of color rather than sprinkling individual plants here and there throughout your yard. It also greatly simplifies matters if you stick with no more

Plume celosias create fireworks in a bed that also features red salvia and blue ageratum. All three are easy annuals that thrive with little care in warm summer weather.

than three different species in a given year. Don't worry. Most bedding flowers are annuals that grow for only one season, so you will have plenty of chances to try different species in future years.

When planting a large area, you may be surprised at how many plants you need. Look on plant tags to see how much space each plant requires.

Watch Out!
Rootbound Bedders

If you see tangled roots growing out through the drainage holes of a cell-pack, it's a sign that the plants are badly crowded. If possible, opt for younger plants that have not been waiting as long for a home. They will transplant better and bloom longer and stronger too.

Gently break apart the lowest roots of bedding plants as you transplant them. This step encourages the development of vigorous new roots.

Tips for Easy Transplanting

- Keep bedding plants constantly moist until you get them situated in beds or containers.

- Dig beds at least 12 inches deep, and mix in an organic or timed-release fertilizer according to label directions.

- Squeeze seedling containers from the bottom to free plants rather than trying to pull them out by the stem.

- Untangle the bottom half-inch of roots if they are matted together. If the roots are severely knotted, break them apart with your fingers and set the plant in the ground with its butterflied bottom spread as wide as possible.

- After the planting is done, water thoroughly, and top the bed with a 2-inch-thick blanket of mulch.

The Need To Feed

As spring ends and summer gets cooking, annual flowers often need a booster feeding to keep them growing strong. You can sprinkle a little organic or granular fertilizer over the soil around plants, or use a plant food that you mix with water. If plants perk up after a booster feeding with a liquid, you will know they were in need of nutrients.

A blanket of mulch looks attractive, and plants benefit from the way mulch conserves water and discourages weeds.

Try These
Fifteen Fine Bedders

- **Ageratum** – Blue or white powder-puff blossoms on low, mound-forming plants. Full sun to partial shade.

- **Begonia** – Pink, red or white flowers on petite plants, some with bronze leaves. Full sun to partial shade.

- **Celosia** – Feathery plumes or convoluted crowns in bright reds, yellows and rusty orange tones. Full sun.

- **Dusty miller** – Soft gray foliage goes with everything and is outstanding with blue or pink flowers. Best in partial shade.

- **Geranium** – Red and white are most common, but pinks are available too. Needs great drainage, best in almost-full sun.

- **Impatiens** – Huge range of colors and a strong preference for shade make this a sure bet for outdoor living areas. Needs plenty of water.

- **Lobelia** – Hundreds of deep blue or white flowers on small spreading plants make this a great texture plant or edging. Best in full sun in cool climates.

- **Marigold, French** – These are the small or dwarf marigolds with flowers only 1 to 2 inches across. Nonstop bloomers, best in full sun.

Ageratum.

Celosia.

- **Melampodium** – Plants stay covered with dozens of little orange-yellow daisies through the hottest weather. Full sun.

- **Pansy** – Best color flower for cool weather, with an extremely long bloom time and wide range of colors. Full sun to partial shade.

- **Petunia** – Versatile, elegant and eager to bloom, petunias are unbeatable for beds, window boxes or other containers in sun or partial shade.

- **Salvia** – Upstanding and large, bright red salvia spikes can fire up partial shade, or you can use blue species in sunnier sites.

- **Verbena** – Annual verbenas bear clusters of richly colored flowers, and there are softer hues as well. Best in full sun.

- **Vinca, annual** – Often called periwinkle or Madagascar periwinkle, this white, pink or purple bloomer thrives in hot weather and full sun.

- **Zinnia** – Always cheery and easy to grow, zinnias are at home in any sunny spot. Check out the different types, which become more numerous every year.

PROCURING PERENNIAL PLANTS

Take some care to choose healthy and vibrant perennial stock. Here's how.

One of the blessings (or banes, if your garden is already overflowing) of today's gardening is the ever-increasing selection of well-grown perennials available at local garden centers.

Among the more provident aspects of early 21st-century life is the availability of goods, be they exotic cooking ingredients or the newest—or oldest—varieties of perennials. Gone are the days when only a handful of local nurseries offered perennials and the number of mail-order sources was limited. Today, perennials are widely offered for sale, from a basic selection at discount department stores in spring, to vastly stocked local garden centers and a staggering number of mail-order companies.

Each of these sources has advantages and disadvantages. Inveterate shoppers will revel in the possibilities, making the most of any and all possible sources for procuring perennials to use in every nook and cranny of the yard.

Merchants

For several months during the spring, hardware stores, home supply stores and discount department stores bring in plants for sale. Annuals are their bread and butter, and the perennials they offer are usually limited to the most common—and easily propagated—types growing in 4-inch or 1-gallon pots. If you need to buy in quantity for a mass planting, these places may prove a good source. The key is to get the plants soon after they arrive, before they've sat too long in the hot sun with infrequent watering. The real fun of shopping at these places is the adventure of finding something special. If you're the kind of person who likes to stop at yard sales, hoping to discover a genuine cameo for 50 cents, then this is your milieu.

Depending on their focus, local nurseries and garden centers can range from offering little better than the mass merchandisers to having a wide range of perennials. Do your own personal research and talk with other gardeners in your area for suggestions of the best places. Again, plants are mainly available in 4-inch or 1-gallon pots.

Container-grown plants in this size pot are usually old enough to bloom

Local garden centers that specialize in perennials enable gardeners to select from among a wide range of varieties and sizes.

the first season. Look for plants that are bushy and compact, with healthy green foliage and no signs of insects or disease. Plants that seem over-sized for the container are most likely root bound, which can cause them to be slower in getting established in your garden.

Small Providers

Another local source that can be invaluable is gardeners who have gotten bitten by the gardening bug so badly that, as their gardens proliferate, they find it sensible to sell some of their extras. Often, these are people who collect and specialize, so it's a good chance to acquire hard-to-find varieties. To find these people, check the classified ads, roadside signs or local plant societies. The plants may be offered bare-root or growing in containers. A variation on this theme are the plant sales and swaps conducted by local plant societies.

Mail-Order

Mail-order sources provide the greatest selection of perennials. These range from mom-and-pop operations to large, long-established corporations. Some companies specialize in certain genera, while others offer the full range of perennials. The plants may be available as seed, dormant bare-root plants, young seedlings or older, larger plants in pots.

Make sure you understand what you're getting before ordering. Most of these companies, especially the smaller ones, are run by people who are dedicated plant enthusiasts and are quite reliable. If you've

never ordered plants by mail or have no first-hand information about the quality offered by a particular company, make your first order a small one.

Those who have ever ordered anything by mail that is even vaguely garden-related are probably already receiving catalogs from some of the major companies. For the smaller companies, you will have to call or mail a request for a catalog, usually including a nominal fee. The offerings may be a simple list or an elaborate catalog with color photos. The catalogs that contain detailed descriptions about the plants are among the most valuable sources of information about perennials.

Gardeners seldom suffer post-Christmas depression because their mailboxes are filled at this time with catalogs for poring over and planning the garden during the long winter nights. Companies ship dormant, bare-root plants in early spring, and container-grown plants are sent at the time of the last expected frost for your area unless requested otherwise.

Both bare-root and container-grown plants are ideally planted as soon as bought or received. Bare-root plants are the most difficult to handle if not planted immediately. They are usually wrapped in moistened packing material and plastic. Left too long in this, the roots will rot. Removed too soon, they will dry out. When planting right away is not possible, unwrap the plants, pot up in containers of potting soil and put in a protected place outdoors. Small seedlings are also best potted up and cared for until they attain some size before planting into the garden.

Young plants, shipped in 4-inch pots, have been carefully packed to arrive in good condition. Open the box immediately and water well, place in indirect light, then plant or repot as soon as possible.

STARTING PERENNIALS

There's a right way and a wrong way to start perennial plants. Here's the right way.

Carefully remove a plant from the container so as not to pull the top from the roots. If the plant is root bound, loosen the root ball with your fingers or cut the sides with a knife.

Preparing the soil before planting is crucial to successfully growing perennials as it's difficult, if not impossible, to improve the soil after perennials are planted. For details on this process, see the Garden Tip on Advance Soil Preparation.

Once both soil and plants are ready, try to plant on a cool, cloudy day when rain is predicted. Late afternoon is the best time to plant as the cool evening gives the plant time to adjust. Try to avoid hot or windy weather. When unavoidable, keep the plant watered and provide protection for several days, such as placing a cardboard box over the plant during the hottest part of the day.

Bare-Root

When planting bare-root perennials, don't let the roots dry out. It's best to soak them for several hours in a weak fertilizer solution. With a trowel or spade, dig a hole large enough for the roots to spread out. Set the plant in the hole so that the point where the roots meet the stem or crown is at ground level. Fill in with soil around the roots, tamping gently, then water thoroughly.

Container-Grown

The boons of container-grown plants are that they are already actively growing and, with a caveat, they can be planted any time during the growing season. Planting in spring, near or after the last frost, depending on the hardiness of the plant, is still the best time because the cool spring weather gives the plant time to establish new roots before hot weather, and it probably has not become root bound yet.

When ready to plant a container-grown perennial, dig a hole, grasp the plant at the base near the soil and gently tug it from the pot. If it doesn't easily come out, turn the pot on its side and tap it several times to jar the root ball loose. Use your fingers to loosen the roots slightly. If there is a mass of roots on the outside of the soil ball, free them up even more or slash the sides of the root ball with a knife. This may seem cruel and unusual punishment, but it stimulates new root growth out into the soil. Place the plant in the hole, setting it at the same depth as it was in the pot. Water thoroughly.

Starting from Seed

An idiosyncrasy of people new to gardening is the desire to start plants from seed. Indeed, there are few processes as miraculous as watching a seed become leaves and flowers, but let's talk reality here. Starting a tomato is one thing; starting a perovskia is another—for a number of reasons.

First of all, perennials are a diverse group of plants, with many different conditions necessary for successful germination.

Second, we're talking delayed gratification. It's usually at least a year before the plants are big enough to set out into the garden, and then they may or may not bloom that year. In the meantime, they must be attended to in a nursery area, including watering them all summer and protecting them during the winter.

Third, perennials are often grown as a specific variety that will not come true from seed but only from vegetative propagation, such as division or cuttings.

Fourth, many perennials multiply quite handily on their own, readily providing new, blooming-size plants.

Garden Tip
Advance Soil Preparation—The Key to Success

Nothing ... nothing is more important to the successful growth of plants than proper advance soil preparation. Skip this all-important first step, and you're asking for trouble. Abide by it, and you've taken a huge step in ensuring a thriving, easy-to-care-for garden.

No matter what type of soil you have, from the lightest sand to the heaviest clay, a liberal addition of organic matter works miracles. Organic matter can be anything from compost to well-rotted leaf mold, fine fir bark or peat moss. Almost every area of the country lays claim to indigenous, inexpensive organic material, readily available to gardeners.

A good rule-of-thumb is that the amount of organic matter you add should be equal to the depth to which you intend to turn the soil. If you're preparing the soil for raised beds, the minimum depth you should till is six inches; eight or 12 inches or more is that much better. This may contradict some traditional advice, but experience has proved it to be very successful.

If you intend to till the soil to a depth of 8 inches, then you should add 8 inches of organic material on top of the soil before you till to incorporate it to the full depth. This takes some doing, but it helps develop an extensive, healthy root system. This results in a hardy, vigorous, productive garden, able to withstand periods of drought and more resistant to disease and pests.

Container-grown plants can be set out anytime during the growing season, but be sure to prepare the soil well before planting, then properly care for the plants afterward.

Depending on what you're planting and the characteristics of your soil, you may want to add fertilizer and lime as you incorporate the organic matter. Explain your situation to your local nursery staff or extension agent to find out if such additions are necessary.

After tilling the organic matter into the soil, rake the area smooth and plant your plants. Keep the area well watered for the first few weeks after planting. You'll be amazed at the growth the plants put on in such superior soil, even in the first year.

But there are times when starting perennials from seed does make sense. For one, maybe you just want to. This may be simple hardheadedness, a need for a great many plants at a reasonable cost or a desire to grow rare plants that do not readily multiply and/or do come true from seed. And some perennials do quickly germinate, grow and bloom the first year if started early enough. These include certain varieties of English daisy, delphinium, shasta daisy and painted daisy.

How to Start from Seed

The procedure for starting perennial seed is much the same as for any other plant. There's a plethora of seed-starting paraphernalia available, but horticultural-grade vermiculite and a plastic seed-starting tray is simple and easy.

Read the instructions on the seed packet to determine whether there are special requirements, such as the need for heat, light, darkness, soaking, cold period or scratching the seed coat. Germination times vary greatly, so keep the growing media moist throughout the waiting period.

Once germinated, provide bright, indirect light, either by growing under fluorescent lights or placing in a greenhouse or lathhouse.

Once several sets of leaves have developed, transplant the seedlings to larger pots or into a nursery bed, if all frost is past. Shelter them with shade cloth or lath or continue growing them in a cool greenhouse or indoors under lights until they start sending out new leaves again.

At this point, the seedlings can be kept growing in pots or set into a nursery bed outdoors. Water and fertilize regularly during the summer. Mulch the nursery bed in late fall after the ground has frozen or cover with a cold frame. The plants should be ready to set into the garden the following spring.

Native Perennial Gardens

Try native perennials for a relaxed, natural and beautiful look.

A native garden is one that contains predominantly native wildflowers in a setting that is as close as possible to the one where they might be found growing in nature. The three most common native gardens are the spring-blooming deciduous woodland garden, the sunny prairie garden and the bog garden, which may be in sun or shade. When considering any of these gardens, the area of your yard to be used should already show a tendency for such a planting. For example, if an area of the yard has trees, then that would likely be an appropriate spot for a woodland garden. If a stream runs through your property, then planting along it with bog-type plants would be appropriate.

In designing native gardens, it's also logical to take your cues from nature. Study the types of areas you want to emulate. Any translation of a wild garden to a cultivated one should be preceded with a study of the trees, shrubs and flowers that naturally grow together. Observe the type of soil, light and moisture of the area where you will develop your wild garden.

When ready, clear the site, prepare the soil carefully and set the plants out just as you would for any new garden area. Do not dig plants from the wild and be sure purchased plants are nursery propagated. Weeding will also be necessary so that the plants you want to spread can do so. It is a fallacy that a native garden does not require planning or maintenance; a garden is a garden, no matter the style.

Try These
Perennials for Woodland Gardens

Actaea rubra
Adiantum pedatum
Aquilegia canadensis
Arisaema triphyllum
Asarum canadense
Asplenium platyneuron
Chrysogonum virginianum
Cimicifuga racemosa
Dentaria spp.
Disporum spp.
Dryopteris spp.
Hepatica spp.
Iris cristata
Jeffersonia diphylla
Mertensia virginica
Phlox divaricata, P. pilosa, P. stolonifera
Podophyllum peltatum
Polemonium reptans
Polystichum acrostichoides
Sanguinaria canadensis
Trillium spp.
Uvularia spp.

Try These
Perennials for Prairie Gardens

Achillea spp.
Agastache spp.
Amsonia tabernaemontana
Andropogon spp.
Asclepias spp.
Aster spp.
Baptisia spp.
Boltonia asteroides
Chrysopsis spp.
Coreopsis spp.
Echinacea spp.
Eryngium yuccifolium
Eupatorium spp.
Filipendula spp.
Gaillardia spp.
Geranium pratense
Helianthus spp.
Heliopsis spp.
Leucanthemum spp.
Liatris spp.
Miscanthus spp.
Monarda spp.
Oenothera spp.
Panicum spp.
Penstemon spp.
Phlox spp.
Ratibida spp.
Rudbeckia spp.
Solidago spp.
Sorghastrum spp.
Thalictrum spp.
Vernonia spp.

PERENNIAL FOLIAGE GARDENS

Foliage can be as pretty as flowers. Here's how to pull it off.

Foliage takes center stage in this planting of grasses with stachys and santolina.

The leaves of perennials are usually thought of as an adjunct to the flowers, but in certain situations, focusing on foliage can have a dramatic effect in the garden. A garden where foliage predominates is more likely to produce a feeling of calmness in the viewer. Sometimes it can mean a garden that requires less maintenance. The stars of the perennial garden based on foliage are the hostas, the ferns and the ornamental grasses. Ferns are the only ones that truly do not produce flowers.

Hostas are the premier foliage plant for shaded situations in the landscape. They grow best in a soil that is rich in organic matter and moist but well drained. Generally, variegated and golden-leaved varieties tolerate more sun than green- or blue-leaved varieties. Some suggested cultivars for various uses in the garden are shown in the sidebar.

Try These
A Hosta Primer

- Dwarf—eight inches or shorter. Best suited for rock gardens or containers.
  Gold-leaved: 'Little Aurora', 'Blonde Elf'
  Green-leaved: 'Baby Bunting', 'Gum Drop'
  White-edged: 'Stiletto', 'Verna Lean'
  Yellow-centered: 'Just So', 'Kabitan'

- Edging—12 inches or shorter. Perfect for the outside edge of a border.
  Green-leaved: 'Snow Flakes', 'Floradora'
  White-edged: 'Aristocrat', 'Ginko Craig'
  Variegated: 'Emerald Tiara', 'Geisha'
  Yellow-edged: 'Scooter', 'Brim Cup'

- Groundcover—20 inches or shorter. Vigorous; good choice for low-maintenance, mass plantings.
  Blue-leaved: 'Blue Wedgwood', 'Halcyon'
  Gold-leaved: 'Midas Touch', 'Day Break'
  Green-leaved: 'Aoki', 'Invincible'
  Variegated: 'Bright Lights', 'Janet'
  White-edged: 'Francee', 'Fair Maiden'
  Yellow-edged: 'Frances Williams', 'Yellow River'

- Background—24 inches or more. Excellent for filling in at the backs of shade beds and borders.
  Blue-leaved: 'Blue Vision', 'Wheaton Blue'
  Gold-leaved: 'Gold Regal', 'Sun Power'
  Green-leaved: 'Royal Standard', 'Honeybells'
  White-edged: 'Antioch', 'Frosted Jade'
  Yellow-edged: 'Wide Brim', 'Pizzaz'

- Specimen—36 to 48 inches. Spectacular plants that make a strong focal point in the garden.
  Blue-leaved: 'Blue Mammoth', 'Krossa Regal'
  Gold-leaved: 'Sum and Substance', 'Golden Medallion'
  Green-leaved: 'Edge of Night', 'Green Wedge'
  White-edged: 'Regal Splendor', 'Crowned Imperial'
  Yellow-edged: 'Sagae', 'Carnival'

Vinca becomes a fine-textured foil to the dramatic clumps of different hosta varieties that invite one to sit upon a bench and enjoy the splendors of the garden.

PERENNIAL GARDENS FOR BUTTERFLIES AND BIRDS

Everyone loves winged visitors in the garden. Here's how to attract them.

Birds and butterflies will make a home in your garden if it provides food, cover, nesting sites and a constant supply of fresh water.

Any garden is a veritable cosmopolitan ecosystem, complete with a full range of animals, insects and birds as well as assorted microorganisms and other critters large and small. Of these, birds and butterflies are among the most desired, particularly for the bright, flitting colors of both and the songs of the birds.

Some people may contend that the birds will feed on the caterpillars as well as bugs and berries, but unless you're trying to nurture a very rare species of butterfly, a balanced population of each can usually be reached. The one thing that you will have to give up, or at least minimize, in this type of garden is pesticides.

The most important aspect of encouraging birds and butterflies to your garden is providing adequate habitat. Birds need plants that will provide food, cover and nesting sites. Nectar plants for adult butterflies are necessary, along with larval food plants for caterpillars. Both birds and butterflies need a constant supply of fresh water.

Try These
Perennials That Use Seeds to Attract Birds

Aster	Papaver
Boltonia	Penstemon
Chrysanthe-mum	Rudbeckia
	Salvia
Coreopsis	Solidago
Echinacea	Spigelia
Echinops	Vernonia
Gaillardia	

Try These
Perennials That Attract Butterflies

For Nectar:	Host Plants for Larvae:
Achillea	
Aster	Artemisia
Centranthus	Asclepias
Coreopsis	Foeniculum
Echinacea	Viola
Eupatorium	
Helianthus	
Hemerocallis	
Liatris	
Lobelia	
Monarda	
Phlox	
Rudbeckia	
Salvia	
Sedum	
Solidago	
Verbena	

Try These
Perennials That Attract Hummingbirds

Aquilegia	Lobelia
Asclepias	Monarda
Heuchera	Penstemon
Iris	Salvia

ROCK GARDENS WITH PERENNIALS

If your soil and space isn't so great, you can still have a pretty garden.

The challenge of creating a rock garden seems of little consequence to those who are drawn to its style and character.

Try These
Perennials for Rock Gardens

Achillea clavennae, A. tomentosa	'Goldfink'
Aquilegia	Dianthus
Arabis	Dicentra
Armeria	Filipendula vulgaris
Artemisia schmidtiana	Gaillardia 'Goblin'
Aruncus aethusifolius	Geum
Asarum	Helianthemum
Aster dumosus	Heuchera
Aubrieta	Iberis
Aurinia	Linum
Bellis perennis	Platycodon grandiflorus 'Apoyame'
Bergenia spp.	Santolina
Campanula—selected spp.	Saponaria
Cerastium	Scabiosa
Coreopsis auriculata 'Nana'	Sedum—selected spp.
Coreopsis grandiflora	Sempervivum
	Teucrium
	Veronica—selected spp.

People can spend years studying and constructing rock gardens. It requires a keen sense of imagination and practical skill to create an area that takes on the effect of a mountain setting. In planning a rock garden, you should choose a site in full sun with excellent drainage, never too close to trees where roots can take over. It's best to use rocks naturally found in your area so that the artificial outcropping you're going to create looks as appropriate as possible. At least some of these rocks should be of a large size, which means you may need the assistance of a contractor to place them with the bottom three-fourths buried. These rocks should be tilted toward the top of the grade to look natural and to channel water into the soil.

There should be deep pockets of soil between the rocks, with the soil mixture usually composed of one-half part garden loam, one-half part humus, one part half-inch crushed rock and one part coarse sand. Often somewhere in the rock garden is a scree, which is a heap of fine stones representing a rock slide or the tip of a glacial moraine. This should be about 12 inches thick, the bottom three inches composed of two- to three-inch stone and the rest a mix-

ture of two parts half-inch crushed rock and one part garden loam. Because of the fast drainage, rock gardens must be watered regularly and deeply, but the soil should never be allowed to remain soggy.

The plants most often used in a rock garden are ones that may naturally grow in such a situation. Otherwise, in choosing plants for a rock garden, consider the size of the garden, the size of the plant, how much it spreads, its growing requirements and how it will look in the overall composition.

The art in developing a rock garden is in having it look as if the rocks "grew" there naturally. Large boulders should be "planted," with only a quarter of them showing.

THE VARIEGATED SHADE GARDEN

Never give up on a shady spot. There are ways to make it gorgeous!

Gardeners complaining that a shade garden seems boring without the bright flowers of the summer border—the petunias in radiant pink and purple shades or the zinnias with fiesta colors—have only to look at the variegated shade garden with plants blooming and leaf colors in much the same brilliance, to realize their error.

The leaves of variegated shade plants come not only in greens and whites, but also with the silver spots of the lungwort, the Persian carpet tones of coleus, the deep burgundy colors of carpet bugle and the cotton candy pink color of wintercreeper 'Emerald Gaiety' in the winter. Even ivy, which a gardener might think of as coming only in a uniform dark green, actually comes in bright limy shades, and rip-roaring yellow edged in green. But just naming these few varieties—what about caladiums and hostas—does an injustice to the vast colorful world of the variegated garden.

Letting Plant Color Define Space

The variegated shade garden reminds us, as gardeners, that we are painters of space and that the plants we set into our garden are as much an aesthetic choice as any artist who lays the first daub of color onto a bare white canvas. As garden artists, we are taking space and pouring in color. Green, with its soothing, calming effect, pleases us and seems a neutral backdrop—an undercoat in painting parlance—to the

Just a sample of the stunning leaf patterns a variegated garden offers.

color touches that accent and highlight the rest of our garden borders. One of the wonderfully complicating factors—which is why gardening is anything but boring—is that the palette changes continuously with the seasons, and our living "painting" subtly changes as one day flows into another.

Choosing variegated leaves lets the shade border shimmer with color. Remember the design principle that bright, light colors seem closer than the dark colors. Assess your planting space critically. If there seems to be a dark hole at the end of the garden, then planting variegated plants will set it alive with color and light, accenting and highlighting the area. If you want to make a small space seem bigger, choose plants with dark-colored leaves, in tones of deep purples, bur-

Even used singly, coleus makes an impressive display. When planted together, with a variety of colors and patterns, the Persian carpet effect is dazzling.

gundy or bronze such as the dark-toned cultivars of coral bells. To make the space appear to be light and filled with color, use plants with leaves that are light golden-yellow or lime green.

The end of a walkway is the perfect spot for an explosion of color from variegated plants. You can lead up to this focal point with contrasting or coordinating colors in the border, or use all green to provide a dramatic buildup to the variegated plants at the end of the walk.

Try These
Perennials for Dry Soil and Shade

The soil under large trees and shrubs is often especially dry and, because of the competition from roots, low in nutrients. Growing perennials in this situation is difficult, but several plants tolerate this situation. Even so, it's important to incorporate organic matter and fertilizer into the soil before planting and to water regularly.

Alchemilla	Pulmonaria
Convallaria	Stachys
Epimedium	Symphytum
Galium	Tricyrtis
Lamium	Vinca

Try These
Perennials for Moist Soil and Partial Shade

A wide range of perennials will thrive in locations with partial (not deep) shade and moist but well-drained soil.

Acanthus	Chelone	Helleborus	Polygonatum
Aconitum	Cimicifuga	Heuchera	Pulmonaria
Ajuga	Convallaria	Heucherella	Ranunculus
Alchemilla	Corydalis	Hosta	Sanguinaria
Aquilegia	Dicentra	Lamium	Symphytum
Artemisia	Digitalis	Ligularia	Thalictrum
Aruncus	Doronicum	Liriope	Tiarella
Asarum	Epimedium	Lobelia	Tricyrtis
Astilbe	Filipendula	Monarda	Vinca
Bergenia	Galium	Nepeta	Viola
Brunnera	Gaura	Oenothera	Waldsteinia
Campanula	Geranium	Phlox (some)	
Carex	Hakonechloa	Polemonium	

SPRING

ENTERTAINING

In spring, the last thing you want to do is spend hours slaving in a hot kitchen. Yet, with all the reasons to celebrate — from Easter dinner to a spring shower, from an elegant brunch to a sit-down dinner party, even Cinco de Mayo (what a great reason to gather!) — you still want to entertain family and friends in style. Here are the ideas you need to pull it all off in delicious style ... and still have time to enjoy the occasion.

Facing page: Smoked Almond Quesadillas, page 158

ANY OCCASION SPRING SHOWER

Whether it's an engagement, bridal or baby shower, this is a very engaging menu. Even with no showers in sight, this menu makes a delightful luncheon for any occasion.

Menu

~ Herbed Coeur à la Crème
~ Figs Stuffed with Walnut Cream Cheese
~ Chutney Chicken Salad with Hazelnuts
~ Sparkling Ginger Fruit Punch
~ Lacy Crisps

Entertains 8.

Herbed Coeur à la Crème

A heart-shaped mold elevates this tasty cream cheese spread to an elegant party dish. You can get the traditional porcelain mold at most gourmet shops, but any glass, plastic or metal heart-shaped mold will do.

2   (8-oz.) pkg. cream cheese, softened
2   green onions, minced
1   garlic clove, minced
½   teaspoon lemon juice
1   tablespoon *herbes de Provence*

1 In medium bowl, combine cream cheese, green onions, garlic, lemon juice and *herbes de Provence*; blend until well mixed.

2 Line 2-cup heart-shaped mold or bowl with cheesecloth; press cream cheese mixture into mold. Chill about 30 minutes or until ready to use. Unmold cheese; remove cheesecloth. Place cheese on serving platter. Surround with toast triangles or heart-shaped crackers.

8 servings.
Preparation time: 5 minutes.
Ready to serve: 30 minutes.
Per serving: 200 calories, 19.5 g total fat (12.5 g saturated fat), 60 mg cholesterol, 170 mg sodium, 0 g fiber.

Before the Event

Make the herbed cream a day ahead. Press it into a mold lined with cheesecloth, then refrigerate.

FIGS STUFFED WITH WALNUT CREAM CHEESE

This appetizer works best with dried figs that are still plump and moist. It is also delicious with dried Mediterranean apricots or dates.

1   (8-oz.) pkg. cream cheese, softened
¼   cup finely chopped toasted walnuts*
12   large dried figs, cut in half or 12 fresh figs, quartered

1 In medium bowl, combine cream cheese and walnuts; mix well. Spoon cream cheese mixture into fig halves.

8 servings.
Preparation time: 15 minutes.
Ready to serve: 15 minutes.
Per serving: 200 calories, 12.5 g total fat (6.5 g saturated fat), 30 mg cholesterol, 90 mg sodium, 3 g fiber.

Menu Tip
- To toast walnuts, spread on baking sheet; bake at 375°F for 7 to 10 minutes or until lightly browned. Cool.

Before the Event
Make the walnut cream cheese a day ahead, cover and refrigerate.

CHICKEN CHUTNEY SALAD WITH HAZELNUTS

Chutney is a wonderful condiment, and the fruit varieties available go way beyond the traditional mango.

4	cups diced cooked chicken
¾	cup chutney
⅓	cup olive oil
1	tablespoon balsamic vinegar
¾	cup chopped toasted hazelnuts*
8	cups mixed greens

1 In large bowl, combine chicken, chutney, oil, vinegar and hazelnuts; stir until well combined.

2 Serve mixture over bed of greens.

8 servings.
Preparation time: 15 minutes.
Ready to serve: 15 minutes.

Per serving: 310 calories, 20 g total fat (3 g saturated fat), 55 mg cholesterol, 85 mg sodium, 2 g fiber.

Menu Tip

- To toast hazelnuts, spread on baking sheet; bake at 375°F about 10 minutes or until lightly browned. Cool.

Before the Event

Mix the chicken chutney a day ahead, cover and refrigerate.

SPARKLING GINGER FRUIT PUNCH

Ginger ale gives this fruit punch an extra kick.

1   quart pineapple juice, chilled
1   quart orange juice, chilled
2   quarts gingcr alc, chilled
    Ice

1 In large punch bowl, combine pineapple juice, orange juice and ginger ale. Add ice before serving.

8 servings.
Preparation time: 5 minutes.
Ready to serve: 35 minutes.
Per serving: 225 calories, 0 g total fat (0 g saturated fat), 0 mg cholesterol, 30 mg sodium, 5 g fiber.

Before the Event

Make several trays of ice cubes using ginger ale. This will cool the punch without diluting it.

LACY CRISPS

These cookies come out of the oven bubbling and too soft to remove from the parchment.

Wait a few minutes until they're firm, with a thin and crispy consistency.

¼ cup all-purpose flour
¼ teaspoon ground ginger
⅛ teaspoon salt
2 tablespoons unsalted butter, softened
¼ cup packed light brown sugar
2 tablespoons light corn syrup
2 tablespoons finely chopped almonds

Before the Event

Make cookie dough ahead, then freeze or refrigerate until you're ready to bake. Store baked cookies in an airtight container.

1 Heat oven to 375°F. Line baking sheet with parchment paper.

2 In medium bowl, combine flour, ginger, salt, butter, brown sugar, corn syrup and almonds; mix well.

3 Divide dough evenly into 16 small balls; arrange about 3 inches apart on baking sheet. Bake 5 to 7 minutes or until light golden around edges and bubbling.

4 Cool cookies on baking sheet about 2 minutes or until cookies harden. Remove cookies from parchment to serve.

8 servings.
Preparation time: 5 minutes.
Ready to serve: 12 minutes.
Per serving: 95 calories, 4 g total fat (2 g saturated fat), 8 mg cholesterol, 45 mg sodium, 0 g fiber.

CELEBRATE CINCO DE MAYO

Mexican Independence Day is a perfect excuse to indulge in enticing foods from south of the border. It's a springtime celebration ... with foods suited to the season!

Menu

~ Smoked Almond Quesadillas
~ Fresh Pineapple Salsa
~ Tijuana Shrimp with Corn Tortillas
~ Sweet Tortilla Triangles
~ Dulce con Leche Ice Cream

Entertains 6.

SMOKED ALMOND QUESADILLAS

Quesadillas are really Mexican grilled cheese sandwiches. Smoked almonds give these simple appetizers a real flavor punch.

¾ cup chopped smoked almonds
1 cup (4 oz.) grated Monterey Jack cheese
12 (8-inch) flour tortillas
2 tablespoons vegetable oil
2 cups tomato salsa

Before the Event

Assemble the quesadillas a day ahead, then cover and refrigerate until you're ready to grill.

1 Place about 1 tablespoon each of chopped almonds and cheese on half of each tortilla. Fold each tortilla in half; brush both sides with oil.

2 Heat large nonstick skillet over medium-high heat; add tortilla. Warm tortilla about 2 minutes per side or until golden. Remove tortilla from pan; slice into 6 wedges. Repeat with remaining tortillas. Serve with salsa.

Serves 6.
Preparation time: 15 minutes.
Ready to serve: 30 minutes.
Per serving: 505 calories, 25.5 g total fat (6 g saturated fat), 20 mg cholesterol, 875 mg sodium, 6 g fiber.

FRESH PINEAPPLE SALSA

This easy, refreshing salsa helps take some of the heat out of the chipotle peppers in

Tijuana Shrimp (page 160).

3 cups diced fresh pineapple
⅓ cup finely chopped red onion
3 tablespoons chopped fresh mint

Before the Event

Make *Fresh Pineapple Salsa* a day ahead, then cover and refrigerate it.

1 In medium bowl, combine pineapple, onion and mint; mix well. Serve with *Tijuana Shrimp with Corn Tortillas* (page 160).

Serves 6.
Preparation time: 15 minutes.
Ready to serve: 15 minutes.
Per serving: 40 calories, 0.5 g total fat (0 g saturated fat), 0 mg cholesterol, 1 mg sodium, 1 g fiber.

Tijuana Shrimp with Corn Tortillas

Chipotle peppers are smoked jalapeño chiles, and they really generate smoky heat. The salsa and lettuce in this recipe help cool the fire. If you think the heat will be too intense, try substituting about ⅓ cup smoky barbecue sauce for the chipotle pepper.

¼	cup (½ stick) butter
1½	lb. shelled, deveined uncooked jumbo shrimp
3	tablespoons packed brown sugar
1	chopped chipotle pepper in 1 tablespoon adobo sauce
8	cups shredded iceberg lettuce
12	(6½-inch) warm corn tortillas

1 In large skillet, heat butter over medium-high heat until melted. Add shrimp, brown sugar and chipotle pepper. Cook, stirring frequently, 4 to 6 minutes or until shrimp is firm and turns pink.

2 To serve, place lettuce on large platter. Top with shrimp and *Fresh Pineapple Salsa* (page 159); serve with tortillas.

Serves 6.
Preparation time: 10 minutes.
Ready to serve: 16 minutes.
Per serving: 300 calories, 10 g total fat (5.5 g saturated fat), 185 mg cholesterol, 435 mg sodium, 3.5 g fiber.

Before the Event

Clean and devein the shrimp a day ahead, then refrigerate until you're ready to sauté them.

SWEET TORTILLA TRIANGLES

You could call these triangles the Mexican equivalent of crispy cinnamon toast.

3 tablespoons sugar
1 teaspoon ground cinnamon
4 (8-inch) flour tortillas, each cut into 6 wedges
2 tablespoons butter, melted

Before the Event

Make *Sweet Tortilla Triangles* ahead of time and store them in an airtight container until ready to serve.

1 Heat broiler.

2 In small bowl, combine sugar and cinnamon.

3 Brush both sides of tortilla wedges with melted butter; sprinkle both sides with cinnamon-sugar.

4 Place tortilla wedges on baking sheet; place in broiler about 4 inches from heat. Broil 1 minute per side or until golden brown. Serve with scoop of *Dulce con Leche Ice Cream*, as pictured.

Serves 6.
Preparation time: 10 minutes.
Ready to serve: 12 minutes.
Per serving: 150 calories, 6 g total fat (2.5 g saturated fat), 10 mg cholesterol, 160 mg sodium, 1 g fiber.

DULCE CON LECHE ICE CREAM

A rich caramel flavor, very popular in Mexico, permeates this ice cream.

½ cup caramel ice cream topping
1 quart vanilla ice cream, softened

Before the Event

Make *Dulce con Leche Ice Cream* a day ahead and freeze.

1 Swirl caramel into ice cream. Cover; freeze until firm.

Serves 6.
Preparation time: 5 minutes.
Ready to serve: 30 minutes.
Per serving: 245 calories, 10 g total fat (6 g saturated fat), 40 mg cholesterol, 165 mg sodium, 0 g fiber.

ELEGANT SPRING BRUNCH

Spring is in the air, and there's no better way to celebrate than with a beautiful and taste-filled brunch. If brunch isn't in your plan, go right ahead and call this a lunch. Either way it's light, great and full of taste.

Menu

~ Spring Spinach Salad with Candied Pecans
~ Curried Deviled Eggs
~ Roasted Asparagus
~ Salmon Benedict with Lemon Dill Sauce
~ Individual Macaroon Tarts with Lemon Curd

Entertains 6.

Spring Spinach Salad with Candied Pecans

You may want to make a double batch of the pecans in this recipe; they have a way of

disappearing before they get to the salad!

⅓   cup packed brown sugar
6   tablespoons olive oil
3   tablespoons balsamic vinegar
1   cup pecans
6   oz. baby spinach
2   cups sliced fresh strawberries (¼ inch thick)

Before the Event
Make candied pecans a day ahead.

1 In large saucepan, heat ¼ cup of the brown sugar, 1 tablespoon of the oil and 1 tablespoon of the vinegar over medium heat about 1 minute or until syrup bubbles.

2 Add pecans to saucepan; mix to coat. Stir pecans about 4 minutes or until toasted and evenly coated, being careful not to burn. Place sugared pecans on sheet of aluminum foil coated with nonstick cooking spray; carefully separate nuts. Cool completely.

3 In small bowl, whisk together remaining brown sugar, remaining oil and remaining vinegar. Place spinach in large salad bowl; drizzle with dressing. Top with strawberries and pecans.

Serves 6.
Preparation time: 15 minutes.
Ready to serve: 20 minutes.
Per serving: 310 calories, 26 g total fat (3 g saturated fat), 0 mg cholesterol, 30 mg sodium, 3.5 g fiber.

CURRIED DEVILED EGGS

Curry and chutney update this standard appetizer, creating an all-new and exciting taste.

6 hard-cooked eggs, cooled, shelled, halved lengthwise
3 tablespoons mayonnaise
1 tablespoon chopped mango chutney
1 teaspoon vinegar
½ teaspoon curry powder

Before the Event

Cook *Curried Deviled Eggs* a day ahead and refrigerate.

1 Leaving egg whites intact, gently remove yolks.

2 In medium bowl, mash yolks with fork. Stir in mayonnaise, chutney, vinegar and curry powder. Spoon rounded tablespoonfuls of mixture into each egg white half, or pipe mixture with large star tip. Cover with plastic wrap; chill. Remove from refrigerator 30 minutes before serving.

Serves 6.
Preparation time: 20 minutes.
Ready to serve: 30 minutes.
Per serving: 130 calories, 10.5 g total fat (2.5 g saturated fat), 215 mg cholesterol, 105 mg sodium, 0 g fiber.

ROASTED ASPARAGUS

Asparagus means spring is truly here. Roasting brings out asparagus's intense flavor.

2   lb. asparagus
1   tablespoon olive oil
2   tablespoons sesame seeds, lightly toasted*

1 Heat oven to 500°F.

2 In large, shallow baking dish, toss asparagus with oil. Bake, stirring after 3 minutes, about 9 minutes or until asparagus is just tender. Sprinkle with sesame seeds.

Serves 6.
Preparation time: 5 minutes.
Ready to serve: 17 minutes.
Per serving: 75 calories, 4.5 g total fat (0.5 g saturated fat), 0 mg cholesterol, 5 mg sodium, 3 g fiber.

Menu Tip
- To toast sesame seeds, heat small skillet over medium heat. Add sesame seeds; shake skillet continuously until seeds are lightly browned, 3 to 4 minutes.

Before the Event
Earlier in the day, steam the asparagus until tender but crisp. Toss with sesame oil and seeds and microwave on High 1 minute to warm through.

SALMON BENEDICT WITH LEMON DILL SAUCE

The lemon sauce in this benedict is delicious and easier to make than the more traditional hollandaise.

6 (4-oz.) salmon fillets
1 tablespoon olive oil
6 English muffins, halved, toasted
2 cups cream
2 tablespoons lemon juice
1 tablespoon cornstarch
1 teaspoon dill weed plus more to taste

1 Heat oven to 350°F.

2 Place salmon on baking sheet; brush with oil. Bake 10 minutes or until fish flakes easily with a fork.

3 Place each warm salmon fillet on 2 English muffin halves.

4 In medium saucepan, heat cream over medium heat. Meanwhile, in small bowl, combine lemon juice, cornstarch and 1 teaspoon of the dill; mix well. Add lemon juice mixture to saucepan.

5 Bring mixture to a boil, stirring constantly about 6 minutes or until thickened. Season to taste with additional dill. Spoon mixture over salmon.

Serves 6.
Preparation time: 10 minutes.
Ready to serve: 20 minutes.
Per serving: 555 calories, 34.5 g total fat (17.5 g saturated fat), 160 mg cholesterol, 360 mg sodium, 1.5 g fiber.

Before the Event
Bake salmon a day ahead and refrigerate. Cover and warm it through before serving.

INDIVIDUAL MACAROON TARTS WITH LEMON CURD

The mini-muffin tins that help form the tart shells are easy to find in many stores, including groceries. These mini tins come in very handy.

1 cup flaked sweetened coconut
¼ cup powdered sugar
3 tablespoons all-purpose flour
½ teaspoon vanilla extract
1 egg white
1½ cups prepared lemon curd*

Menu Tip
- Prepared lemon curd is available in the jam and jelly section of most grocery stores.

Before the Event
Bake the tart shells one day ahead and store at room temperature.

1 Heat oven to 400°F.

2 In medium bowl, combine coconut, sugar, flour, vanilla and egg white; mix well.

3 Coat miniature muffin tin with nonstick cooking spray. Divide coconut mixture evenly into and up sides of 12 miniature muffin cups, about 2 tablespoons each.

4 Bake 11 to 13 minutes or until golden brown. Cool on wire rack; remove from pan. Cool completely.

5 Top each tart with 2 tablespoons lemon curd.

Serves 6.
Preparation time: 10 minutes.
Ready to serve: 25 minutes.
Per serving: 265 calories, 10 g total fat (5 g saturated fat), 0 mg cholesterol, 105 mg sodium, 1 g fiber.

SPRINGTIME DINNER PARTY

Whether you're celebrating a birthday, graduation, promotion or just a lovely spring day, this dinner will make the occasion perfect — and perfectly delicious. What's even better: Everything tastes like you cooked for hours.

Menu

~ Smoked Trout and Pear Salad
~ Champagne Vinaigrette
~ Creamy Polenta
~ Seared Tenderloin with Mushrooms and Gorgonzola
~ Lime Peas in Tomato Cups
~ Black Forest Cherries Jubilee

Entertains 8.

SMOKED TROUT AND PEAR SALAD

Juicy, ripe pears and salty smoked trout may seem like an odd pairing, but the combination

is unbelievably good.

8 cups baby greens or Boston lettuce
1 recipe prepared *Champagne Vinaigrette*
8 oz. smoked trout, boned, skinned, broken
   into pieces
4 medium ripe pears, peeled, cored, sliced

1 In large bowl, toss greens with ¼ cup of the *Champagne Vinaigrette.*

2 Arrange 1 cup of the greens on each salad plate; top greens with trout and sliced pears.

3 Drizzle plates with remaining *Champagne Vinaigrette*; serve.

Serves 8.
Preparation time: 10 minutes.
Ready to serve: 15 minutes.
Per serving: 210 calories, 15 g total fat (1.5 g saturated fat), 6.5 mg cholesterol, 265 mg sodium, 3 g fiber.

Before the Event
Slice pears earlier in the day and soak in the *Champagne Vinaigrette* to marinate.

CHAMPAGNE VINAIGRETTE

Champagne vinegar adds extra sparkle to this dressing, but white wine vinegar makes a

fine substitute.

3 tablespoons Champagne vinegar
¼ cup hazelnut oil
¼ cup olive oil
   Grated peel of 1 lemon
⅛ teaspoon salt
⅛ teaspoon freshly ground pepper
¼ cup chopped fresh parsley

1 In large bowl, combine vinegar, hazelnut and olive oils, lemon peel, salt and pepper; whisk until well blended. Mix in parsley.

Serves 8.
Preparation time: 5 minutes.
Ready to serve: 5 minutes.
Per serving: 120 calories, 13.5 g total fat (1.5 g saturated fat), 0 mg cholesterol, 35 mg sodium, 0 g fiber.

Before the Event
Make *Champagne Vinaigrette* a day ahead.

CREAMY POLENTA

Polenta is the Italian version of what your grandmother may have called cornmeal mush.

As with many Italian dishes, it is very popular stateside.

8 cups water
2 cups yellow cornmeal
2 teaspoons salt

1 In large pot, combine water, cornmeal and salt; whisk to blend. Bring mixture to a boil over medium-high heat, whisking constantly. Reduce heat to low. Cook about 15 minutes, stirring frequently, until mixture has thickened. Serve with *Seared Tenderloin with Mushrooms and Gorgonzola* (page 177).

Serves 8.
Preparation time: 15 minutes.
Ready to serve: 15 minutes.
Per serving: 125 calories, 0.5 g total fat (1 g saturated fat), 0 mg cholesterol, 585 mg sodium, 2.5 g fiber.

Before the Event
Make *Creamy Polenta* earlier in the day and reheat with ½ cup water before serving.

SEARED TENDERLOIN WITH MUSHROOMS AND GORGONZOLA

The rich flavors in this dish make it a perfect meal for any special occasion or just for treating yourself and a few guests.

8   (4-oz.) tenderloin medallions
1   teaspoon salt
1   teaspoon freshly ground pepper
2   tablespoons butter
¼   cup chopped shallots
2   lb. mixed domestic and wild fresh mush-
      rooms, sliced
1   cup port wine
1   cup reduced-sodium chicken broth
8   oz. Gorgonzola cheese, crumbled

1 Pound medallions until they are ¼ inch thick; season with salt and pepper.

2 In large skillet, heat butter over medium-high heat until melted. Add medallions; sear about 1 minute per side or until cooked to desired doneness. Remove medallions to large plate; cover loosely with aluminum foil to keep warm.

3 Meanwhile, add shallots and mushrooms to skillet; sauté, stirring frequently, about 5 minutes or until liquid evaporates and mushrooms are brown. Add port; simmer 1 minute. Add chicken broth; simmer an additional 4 minutes.

4 To serve: Place each medallion on mound of *Creamy Polenta* (page 176). Pour mushroom mixture over medallions; sprinkle with Gorgonzola.

Serves 8.
Preparation time: 25 minutes.
Ready to serve: 30 minutes.
Per serving: 365 calories, 20 g total fat (10 g saturated fat), 95 mg cholesterol, 830 mg sodium, 1.5 g fiber.

Before the Event
Flatten tenderloins earlier in the day. Slice mushrooms earlier in the day.

LIME PEAS IN TOMATO CUPS

These red tomato cups, filled with bright green peas flavored with a hint of lime, add a flash of lovely color to the plate.

8   medium tomatoes
2   (9-oz.) pkg. frozen baby peas, thawed
2   tablespoons water
6   tablespoons butter
     Grated peel of 1 lime

1 Heat oven to 200°F.

2 Halve tomatoes and remove seeds and ribs to form cups. Place tomatoes on baking sheet; heat about 5 minutes.

3 Meanwhile, in medium saucepan, cook peas with water and butter over medium heat about 3 minutes or until peas are warmed through and butter is melted. Add lime peel; toss.

4 Scoop pea mixture into tomatoes; serve.

Serves 8.
Preparation time: 10 minutes.
Ready to serve: 15 minutes.
Per serving: 135 calories, 9 g total fat (5.5 g saturated fat), 25 mg cholesterol, 115 mg sodium, 4 g fiber.

Before the Event
Prepare the tomatoes earlier in the day.

BLACK FOREST CHERRIES JUBILEE

When you have good-quality canned cherries in your pantry, you are always within

minutes of a great dessert like this one.

2   (15.5-oz.) cans black cherries with juice
⅓   cup cherry brandy
2   teaspoons cornstarch
6   oz. semisweet chocolate, chopped
1   cup cream
2   pints vanilla ice cream

Before the Event

Make cherries and chocolate sauce ahead and
warm through before serving.

1 In medium saucepan, combine cherries, cherry brandy and cornstarch over medium heat; cook about 4 minutes or until juice thickens.

2 Meanwhile, in glass bowl, combine chocolate and cream; microwave on High 1 minute. Stir mixture until chocolate is melted.

3 Place warm cherries with sauce over scoops of ice cream; top with chocolate sauce to taste.

Serves 8.
Preparation time: 5 minutes.
Ready to serve: 10 minutes.
Per serving: 410 calories, 25 g total fat (14 g saturated fat), 60 mg cholesterol, 65 mg sodium, 3 g fiber.

EASY AND CASUAL DINNER

Company's coming! But don't panic. This spectacular dinner comes together in practically no time at all. And, if you're looking for an interesting alternative to the traditional Easter dinner ham, here it is.

Menu

~ Cheese Crisps
~ Crispy Crab Cakes with Mixed Greens
~ Chipotle Mayonnaise
~ Angel Hair Pasta with Spinach and Pine Nuts
~ Rustic Rhubarb Strawberry Tart

Entertains 4.

CHEESE CRISPS

Bake plain grated cheese to a deliciously crisp cracker; it's like a miracle! Just try it and you'll believe too.

8 oz. Parmesan cheese, freshly grated

Before the Event

Make *Cheese Crisps* a day ahead and store in an airtight container.

1 Heat oven to 375°F.

2 Line baking sheet with parchment paper. Drop generous tablespoonfuls of grated cheese onto baking sheet, 3 inches apart.

3 Bake 6 to 8 minutes or until golden. Remove crisps from oven. When completely cool, peel from parchment.

Serves 4.
Preparation time: 15 minutes.
Ready to serve: 22 minutes.
Per serving: 260 calories, 17 g total fat (10 g saturated fat), 44.5 mg cholesterol, 1055 mg sodium, 0 g fiber.

CRISPY CRAB CAKES WITH MIXED GREENS

Crab cakes have been a popular restaurant dish for years. But this easy recipe makes them a homemade treat.

12   oz. crabmeat
¼   cup finely diced roasted red bell pepper
¼   cup minced red onion
2   tablespoons capers, rinsed, chopped
1   egg
¼   teaspoon salt
3   cups fresh white bread crumbs
2   tablespoons butter
4   cups mixed greens

Before the Event

Build the crab mixture and form the cakes a day ahead, then cover and refrigerate until ready to cook.

1 In medium bowl, combine crab, roasted pepper, red onion, capers, egg, salt and 1 cup of the bread crumbs; mix well.

2 Form crab mixture into 8 (1-inch-thick) cakes; coat with the remaining 2 cups bread crumbs.

3 In large skillet, heat butter over medium-high heat until melted. Add cakes; brown 4 minutes per side or until golden brown.

4 Place 2 cakes on 1 cup mixed greens. Repeat with remaining cakes and greens. Serve with *Chipotle Mayonnaise*.

Serves 4.
Preparation time: 20 minutes.
Ready to serve: 30 minutes.
Per serving: 250 calories, 9.5 g total fat (4.5 g saturated fat), 15 mg cholesterol, 715 mg sodium, 2 g fiber.

CHIPOTLE MAYONNAISE

Chipotle peppers (smoked, dried jalapeño chiles) give this mayonnaise its zip.

1   cup mayonnaise
1   tablespoon grated lemon peel
1   tablespoon minced canned chipotle peppers
1   teaspoon minced garlic
¼   cup chopped fresh cilantro

Before the Event

Make *Chipotle Mayonnaise* a day ahead.

1 In medium bowl, combine mayonnaise, lemon peel, chipotle peppers, garlic and cilantro; mix well. Serve with *Crispy Crab Cakes with Mixed Greens*.

Serves 4.
Preparation time: 5 minutes.
Ready to serve: 5 minutes.
Per serving: 400 calories, 44 g total fat (6.5 g saturated fat), 35 mg cholesterol, 340 mg sodium, 1 g fiber.

ANGEL HAIR PASTA WITH SPINACH AND PINE NUTS

Angel hair pasta is very thin and cooks quickly. Be careful not to overcook it, or it will turn mushy.

1   (1-lb.) pkg. angel hair pasta
¼   cup (½ stick) butter
2   garlic cloves, minced or thinly sliced
½   teaspoon crushed red pepper
5   oz. fresh spinach, coarsely chopped
½   cup pine nuts, toasted*
1   cup (4 oz.) freshly grated or shaved Parmesan cheese

1 Cook pasta according to package directions; drain.

2 Meanwhile, in large skillet, heat butter over medium-high heat until melted. Add garlic and crushed red pepper; sauté 1 minute. Reduce heat to medium. Add spinach; sauté gently 1 to 2 minutes or until wilted. Add pine nuts and pasta; toss to mix. Sprinkle with Parmesan cheese.

Serves 4.
Preparation time: 15 minutes.
Ready to serve: 20 minutes.
Per serving: 765 calories, 30.5 g total fat (13.5 g saturated fat), 50 mg cholesterol, 1035 mg sodium, 6.5 g fiber.

Menu Tip
- Toast pine nuts in batches in dry skillet. Or place pine nuts in 15x10x1-inch pan; bake at 350°F for 5 minutes or until golden brown, stirring occasionally.

Before the Event
Cook the pasta, drain and rinse with cold water, then store in the refrigerator until you're ready to add it to the saucepan.

RUSTIC RHUBARB STRAWBERRY TART

You don't need a special pan to make this delicious tart the old-fashioned way shown here. If your garden rhubarb isn't up yet, try the frozen variety.

Pastry Dough

1½ cups all-purpose flour
½ cup (1 stick) unsalted butter, cold and cut into slices
¼ teaspoon salt
⅓ cup very cold water

Filling

1 cup thinly sliced fresh rhubarb
1 cup sliced fresh strawberries
¼ cup sugar
1 teaspoon ground cinnamon

Before the Event

Make the *Rustic Rhubarb Strawberry Tart* a day ahead.

1 Heat oven to 400°F.

2 In bowl, mix flour, butter and salt very lightly with pastry blender, so that butter pieces remain visible throughout flour. Add cold water; mix very quickly until dough coheres. Form into round; wrap with plastic wrap. Refrigerate 30 minutes.

3 Roll dough to form 12-inch circle; place on baking sheet. Top dough with rhubarb and strawberry slices, leaving 1-inch border.

4 Sprinkle fruit with sugar and cinnamon. Fold border up over fruit; pinch to seal. Bake 25 minutes or until crust is golden brown.

Serves 4.
Preparation time: 10 minutes.
Ready to serve: 35 minutes.
Per serving: 440 calories, 23.5 g total fat (14.5 g saturated fat), 60 mg cholesterol, 150 mg sodium, 3 g fiber.

INDEX